Aviation's Mr. Sam

DEDICATION
To Marian and Alma

Aviation's Mr. Sam

by JAMES HAGGERTY

AERO PUBLISHERS, INC.

Fallbrook, Cal. 92028

Library of Congress Catalog Card Number

74-78958

ISBN 0-8168-3100-9

Printed and Published in the United States by Aero Publishers, Inc.

FOREWORD

"Mr. Sam" was the title bestowed upon a great American Congressman, Sam Rayburn, a Democrat from the 4th District of Texas who served 25 consecutive terms in the House of Representatives. It was a title that combined affection for a grand gentleman with respect for the accomplishments of the legislator who was Speaker of the House longer than anyone in American history.

The world of aviation has its "Mr. Sam," too, so dubbed by his associates for reasons similar to those that earned Sam Rayburn the appelation. Aviation's Mr. Sam is Samuel J. Solomon, a pioneer of note, a Washington contemporary of Sam Rayburn for half a century. Sam Solomon was also a part-time resident of Texas during one phase of his career, an honorary Texas Colonel on the Governor's Staff and an Admiral of the Texas Navy. In fact, it was during his Texas period that the Mr. Sam tag originated.

The state of aviation today is a monument to the dedicated efforts of the many people who made a contribution to the progress of flight. Due acclaim has been accorded the great pioneers whose giant steps have been the milestones of aviation history. But their exploits, important as they were, constitute only the framework of aviation growth; the whole structure includes the work of many others who built upon the foundations, the largely unsung contributors whose accomplishments, though less spectacular, represent a significant portion of the total effort.

"Mr. Sam" Solomon is one of the latter. His experience embraces more than forty years, dating back to aviation's adolescence. It includes the founding of a major airline, the presidency of that and two others, management of an airport, direction of a wartime training institute, establishment of two postwar training schools and participation in a variety of other ventures related in one way or another to flying.

By virtue of his many important positions, Sam Solomon was frequently in the news, but his accomplishments were written piecemeal. Many of the events in which he played a part are nowhere chronicled and they should properly be recorded. Hence this volume, the story of a full and rewarding career, frequently exhilarating, frequently hectic and ridden with difficulty—"but always fun," to use Mr. Sam's own summation. It is more than a story of one man's experiences; it is a recollection of an exciting period of aviation growth and a profile of many of the people who made it grow, some of them among the most famous names in aviation's annals.

TABLE OF CONTENTS

S. J. "Mr. Sam" Solomon

CHAPTER I

The Solomons of Washington, D.C.

It was on July 11, 1899 that Samuel Joseph Solomon, first offspring of Samuel and Maggie Solomon of Washington, D.C., became the newest member of the human race.

The world of that day was vastly different from the world we know today. The United States had only a third as many people and the flag had but 45 stars. The American worker's average hourly wage was 22 cents. The automobile had been invented and it was rapidly gaining in popularity, but at the turn of the century it was still greatly outnumbered by horsedrawn conveyances. Women wore high-button shoes, floor-length dresses and flowered hats of enormous dimensions. Among the menfolk, the mustache was very much in evidence but the full beard was in decline; the well-dressed man wore detachable celluloid collars and cuffs and never ventured out without a hat, whether silk topper, bowler or straw boater. No one had yet dreamed of television and even the home radio was some years in the future; the telephone was in existence but its use was confined to business or to the homes of the very wealthy—which the Solomons were not.

In the years of Sam Solomon's infancy, Washington was anything but the bustling world capital it later became. It was, rather, a quiet southern town and a small town at that; the populous suburbs that surround the Capital today were undeveloped land and one could "get out in the country" merely by walking a couple of miles.

The Solomons lived in the Southwest section of the town, where D Street intersected Seventh Street, one of the major thoroughfares. On each of the four corners today, there is a massive government office building. In those days the area consisted mostly of blocks of lower-middle-class "row houses," each monotonously similar to its neighbor, their ranks broken by an occasional apartment building. Along D Street, next to a shop on the corner was one such apartment house; the Solomons lived there when Sam was born and Sam Solomon the Elder ran the shop.

The senior Solomon was well known in Southwest Washington. It was he who laid on the annual Fourth of July fireworks display in his neighborhood. A very handsome man, he was something of an athlete and he had a deep interest in all sports, particularly baseball, boxing and horse racing. In the Gay Nineties, he sponsored a Bureau of Engraving baseball team that won a District of Columbia title. He once rode his own horse in a race at Washington's Benning Race Track; the outcome of the event has been lost to the mists of time.

The elder Solomon was active in the art of pugilism as a manager. He enjoyed considerable success as mentor of a Washington lightweight named Kid Sullivan, who in 1904 won the title of "Champion of the South." Solomon was not always so fortunate, however. On one occasion, when he was handling a boxer of little talent and even less heart, Solomon got some first-hand ring experience. His pugilist, feeling that Solomon had overmatched him, decided to be elsewhere on the night of the fight. Sam Solomon, proud of his reputation as a man who lived up to his word, couldn't stand the thought of failing to meet a commitment, so he donned his man's trunks and went into the ring himself. He emerged a badly battered loser, but with pride intact. The experience failed to dim Sam the Elder's enthusiasm for boxing, but he wisely confined his interest thereafter to spectating.

Young Sam's mother, born Maggie Rosenberry, was the daughter of an Irish mother and a Scots-Dutch father. A quiet, gentle woman, she was as pretty as her husband was handsome. Theirs was a mixed marriage, Sam Jewish, Maggie Catholic, but they never let it become a problem. They stayed away from church and synagogue, not because they were irreligious, but because they felt that participating in congregational worship might spark differences where none existed at home.

Early in the Twentieth Century, the Solomon family made its first connection with aviation, a very minor participation, when Sam the Elder made a contribution to help further the experimental work of Samuel Pierpont Langley, architect, mathematician, physicist and one-time Secretary of the Smithsonian Institution.

Aviation in the practical sense did not then exist, but there were many like Langley in the United States and Europe who were laying the foundations for real powered flight. Langley built a full-scale powered airplane called the Aerodrome, designed to be launched by a catapult from a houseboat especially designed for the tests.

In October of 1903 Langley anchored his houseboat in the Potomac River near Widewater, Virginia, and his associate engineer, Charles M. Manly, climbed into the cockpit of the Aerodrome for what both firmly believed would be man's first powered flight. At a signal from Manly, Langley fired the catapult and the Aerodrome began to move. But the launching mechanism fouled and the airplane, moving much too slowly for its wings to gain lift, plunged into the Potomac. Manly extricated himself from the wreckage, wet and shaken but otherwise unhurt.

Undeterred, Langley rebuilt the airplane and readied it for another try two months later. Once again the catapult failed and once again Manly took an unwanted bath in the Potomac. This time the Aerodrome was beyond repair and the experiments ended. For years thereafter Langley's supporters argued that the Aerodrome itself was the first really efficient flying machine and that it could have flown had the catapult worked. It was a moot argument.

Just nine days after the demise of the Aerodrome, on December 17, 1903, came the Great Events that were to have such vast impact on all the peoples of the world and were to influence the direction of young Sam Solomon's future. The events were the first successful trials of a powered flying machine, conducted by a pair of bicycle-makers from Dayton, Ohio, Orville and Wilbur Wright. "Events" is pluralized because, although it is popularly believed that there was only one flight on that memorable day, there were in fact four. Orville and Wilbur took turns at the controls of their frail little biplane, wobbling over the sands of Kill Devil Hills, North Carolina, each flight bettering the duration record of the previous one. On the final flight of the day, Wilbur remained aloft for 59 seconds and soared some 850 feet.

Of course, Sam Solomon knew nothing of this at the time. For one thing, he was barely four years old. But few people of any age learned immediately of the wonderful happenings at Kill Devil Hills. Although the story was telegraphed across the country, most newspapers editors consigned it to the wastebasket; it was clearly the delusion of some lunatic. Only two papers in all the nation ran the account, and their readers, for the most part, smiled at what was obviously an interesting but preposterous hoax.

In 1905, young Sam began his schooling, attending kindergarten and first grade at the Jefferson School in Southwest Washington. Then the growing Solomon family, which by now included Sam's sister Mildred, moved to a new home in Northwest Washington. Another son, Milton, arrived shortly after the move. Still later, Maggie Solomon bore a fourth child, Mary.

Sam's growing-up years at his new school—the Abbott School in Northwest Washington—were pleasant ones. He was a shy youngster, not one to make friends easily, often lonely, but there were a few friends who broke through his reserve. He began to take an interest in sports and he found schoolwork easy; he was far too busy to devote much time to study, but he had that natural ability to absorb learning with a single, quick reading. The only classroom activity that bothered him was group singing. From all accounts, Sam's singing voice was somewhere between a croak and a bleat. It was so bad, in fact, that one of his teachers concluded every group singing assignment with the statement, "And Samuel will not sing."

When he was nine, young Solomon had a thrilling experience—his first view of an airplane in flight. The aviator at the controls was none other than Orville Wright.

For some time after their initial flights, the Wright brothers had sought to sell their flying machine, but with discouraging results. In 1908, however, they were on the threshold of success. They had interested a syndicate in France and the U.S. Army had finally been persuaded—by President Theodore Roosevelt himself—that there might possibly be some military utility in this controversial contraption. By that time the Wrights had two machines, so Wilbur took one to France for a series of exhibitions and Orville undertook to demonstrate the other to the Army.

The Army trials were to be held at Fort Myer, located a few miles from Washington in northern Virginia. The local newspapers carried the story and added that the public would be permitted to watch. It was early September and school had not reopened after the summer recess, so young Sam decided he had to be present at this momentous occasion.

Next day he trudged on foot to the Army camp and joined the spectators scattered around the perimeter of the huge Fort Myer parade ground. It was not a large crowd; by now people had accepted the fact that man could fly but there was general agreement that no good could come of it.

Then, suddenly, the Wright biplane was aloft, soaring high in the sky, or so it seemed to young Sam; years later he learned that the Wright Flyer never topped 300 feet in the Fort Myer trials of 1908. Orville Wright maneuvered the plane through a series of graceful turns around the parade ground, then descended to a gentle landing. It was a magnificent spectacle, one that probably planted a seed in Sam Solomon's subconscious, for some years later he began to talk of becoming an aviator.

When he was 12, Sam joined the YMCA. By now he was firmly in the grip of the athletic urge and the "Y" offered an excellent gymnasium, a basketball court and a swimming pool. More than that, it provided an opportunity to go to summer camp, which Sam did for years thereafter.

That first year marked the beginning of more than 60 years of Sam Solomon's contributions to YMCA programs, including 30 years as a "Y" director. The Y needed new steel rowboats for its summer camp and was trying to raise the money for them. With the help of his mother, Sam became a fund-raiser. Every Friday Maggie Solomon would bake a cake, which Sam would take to the Y on Saturday morning and sell for ten cents a slice, the proceeds going to the rowboat account.

It was about this time that Sam conducted his first experiment in aeronautics, one that many a youngster before and after him has tried with similar results. He climbed a high wall near his home and leaped from it, both hands firmly gripping his parachute—the family umbrella. He learned the hard way that the "parachute" canopy had insufficient lift for the weight it was asked to support. Fortunately, he sustained no limb fractures, but he was a mass of sprains and bruises and he lost all enthusiasm for further parachute research.

It was late in Sam's freshman year in high school that World War I broke out in Europe, but the war, in its initial stages, made little impact on the youth of that day. It was a remote conflagration, separated from the United States by thousands of miles of ocean, hence no matter of concern.

Sam's new educational home was Central High School in Northwest Washington, largest of the District of Columbia's five advanced schools. He enjoyed Central, principally because of the opportunity to participate in organized athletic programs. He tried out for several of the teams—football, swimming, track and even basketball, although he was only a shade above five feet seven; it was a different game in those days and lack of height was not an especial disadvantage. Sam's multi-faceted sports activities naturally widened his circle of acquaintances, and although he was anything but a scholastic social lion, he made more friends than he had as a younger boy.

Sam was a voracious reader and when not in class or on the athletic fields he haunted the public library. His favorite fictional literature was the work of Horatio Alger, the "rags to riches" stories of poor but honest youngsters who planted determined feet on the bottom rung of the ladder and within a hundred pages or so became giants of industry. He read, too, of the real-life accomplishments of the aviation pioneers and his dormant interest in flying was rekindled.

The war brought an opportunity for another close-up look at airplanes. The French, seeking support in the United States, put on a series of flying exhibitions in Washington. At the Polo Grounds adjoining the Potomac River, French pilots demonstrated the Spad, the very latest in military aircraft, a little single-place biplane noted for its maneuverability. Sam Solomon was on hand for each of the demonstrations and it was about this time that he began to talk of becoming an aviator, although he had little idea how to go about it.

Maggie Solomon, who felt that Sam should study to be a lawyer, was dismayed by such nonsensical chatter.

"If God intended man to fly he would have given him wings," she said often. It was not an original remark; in fact, it was the standard rebuttal to aviation enthusiasts. Sam never accepted the premise. After all, man *was* flying, so God must have intended it.

After completing his second year at Central, Sam went off to the YMCA summer camp as usual. He returned early in July to find his mother seriously ill of septicemia. She had, in fact, become ill shortly after Sam left for camp but, characteristically, Maggie Solomon had refused to disrupt Sam's vacation by having him called back home. On Sam's sixteenth birthday, Maggie Solomon died. It was a severe blow. The Solomons were an unusually tight-knit family and the children were passionately devoted to both mother and father. Maggie's passing left a great emptiness.

As Sam continued schooling, through his third and fourth years at Central High, the war that had at first seemed so remote came ever closer. A number of German actions, notably the sinking of the British liner *Lusitania*, in which a large number of Americans lost their lives, outraged the people of the United States. American sympathy swung sharply to the Allied cause and on April 6, 1917, President Woodrow Wilson called for a declaration of war against Germany. There was no dissent on the part of young America; hundreds of thousands immediately volunteered for service against the "hated Hun."

Sam briefly entertained the notion of enlisting in the Marine Corps. He was still under the age limit when he completed his fourth year of high school, but he would become eligible in a month. However, Sam's sense of practicality prevailed over his patriotism. He had, in his senior year, been giving a lot of thought to a career in engineering, aviation or otherwise. But the subjects he had taken in high school were inadequate for enrollment in a collegiate engineering course. He decided to defer military service for a while and take a fifth year at Central to obtain the necessary additional credits.

So instead of going to France in the summer of 1917, Sam went to Oklahoma. Interested in contributing something to the war effort during the summer recess, he learned that a Father O'Grady at Washington's Catholic University was assembling a group of young men to work on Oklahoma's wheat harvest. It was part of a national mobilization effort to maintain agricultural output by replacing the farm workers who were going to war with younger men still not eligible for the Army. This was just what Sam wanted, an opportunity to help the nation while passing an interesting summer recess and making some money in the process. Along with a half dozen others from Central High, he applied and was accepted.

Sam went first to Dover, Oklahoma, where he worked initially as a field hand on a farm, later as a member of a threshing machine crew. It was hard work. In Washington, the youngsters had been told that they would work an eight-hour day. It turned out that that meant eight hours in the morning and eight in the afternoon. For this back-breaking labor, Sam earned less than three dollars a day.

Later in the summer Sam switched to a different type of job, as a laborer in an oil refinery, and still later he transferred again, this time to a construction company building smokestacks in Tulsa. This was even harder work than the wheatfields, repeatedly climbing up the inner structure of the tall stack. The toughest—and somewhat frightening—assignment was whitewashing the completed smokestack, perched precariously on a scaffold at times a hundred feet or more above the ground.

Sam started work on a second smokestack and ran into trouble. Once, especially weary, he decided he simply couldn't make the climb up the structure. Ignoring the regulations, he rode up on a bucket that carried construction materials to the work levels. He paid for his trespass; there was an inexperienced operator running the bucket that day and he hauled it too high, so that both Sam's hands were lacerated by the shivved wheel at the top. Sam was lucky; he lost no fingers. However, he was unable to continue work and he was forced to wind up his Oklahoma stay.

In the fall he returned to Washington and began his final year at Central. It was a triumphant year, both academically and athletically. He played end on the football team, which won every one of its games, one of them by a 120-0 score. He was one of the high scorers on Central's District of Columbia championship basketball team. In swimming, he placed high in the South Atlantic championships. And with the track team he broad-jumped for a gold medal in a national meet. With this all-around performance, Sam Solomon became the first single-year four-letter man in the history of Washington high school athletics.

In June, 1918, Sam graduated from Central. The class year book carried this notation as to the life ambition of Samuel Joseph Solomon: "To be an aviator." In the strict sense of the word, meaning to pilot an airplane, Sam was never to achieve that ambition. In future years, however, he was to become very much a part of the world of aviation.

His schooling concluded, Sam was able to capitalize on his sports prowess by getting a summer job as a swimming instructor. Actually, he had two jobs: he was an instructor at the Community Center pool, which was in Central High School, and he also served as life guard at the District's three municipal swimming pools. Between the two jobs, he was making a great deal of money for that day—about $300 a month.

"What are you doing with all that money?" his father asked him one day.

"Spending it," Sam replied.

The elder Solomon nodded appreciatively.

"Keep it up," he said. "It runs in the family."

In the fall, Sam felt he could no longer stay out of uniform, even though he would have to pass up a scholarship at Lafayette College in order to enlist. He tried first the Marine Corps, but the Marines, foreseeing an early end to the war, had closed enlistments. The Army, however, welcomed him. In September, 1918, he became Private Sam Solomon and was assigned to the Student Army Training Corps, stationed, oddly enough, at Lafayette College, where he might have gone as a collegian.

Sam's stay at Lafayette was a brief one. Ever ambitious, he applied immediately upon arrival for Officers Training School and was accepted. He was transferred to Camp Zachary Taylor at Louisville, Kentucky, for the wartime 90-day course involving a variety of classroom subjects, basic military training and instruction in field artillery tactics.

Halfway through the course the war ended and the trainees were given an option: return home immediately with an honorable discharge or remain for the completion of the 90-day program. Never one to quit something he had started, Sam stayed on at Camp Taylor until January, 1919, when he was commissioned a second lieutenant in the Field Artillery Reserve and simultaneously mustered out of the service.

CHAPTER II
The Swimming Pool Story

The city of Washington, D.C. to which Sam Solomon returned early in 1919 was vastly different from the Washington of his childhood. By now automotive vehicles had almost entirely supplanted the horse and the quiet southern town had become a bustling metropolis spreading outward in all directions from its hub.

Like the city, the Federal government was mushrooming. The end of World War I had brought about the closing of many temporary offices, but for each bureau terminated two new ones sprang into existence, an expansion stimulated partly by the exigencies of postwar readjustment and partly by the managerial demands of a rapidly growing nation.

Sam Solomon became a part of the burgeoning Federal government. He found employment in the Treasury Department, in a section responsible for paying interest on the Liberty bonds which the government had sold to help finance the war effort. It was not an exciting job and neither was it munificent; he started at a hundred dollars a month. Sam, not yet 20, had visions of something better, but he was uncertain as to the nature of his real career and how to pursue it. Treasury, at least, served as a temporary refuge and it offered potentially valuable experience in finance and accounting.

The Treasury period proved very important in another respect. It was soon after he joined the Department that he met Alma Marie Garber, a petite, blonde young lady of obvious intelligence and ability, since she was already a Treasury unit chief. They began regular dating, or "going steady" in the parlance of the day, and in a very brief time Sam decided that Alma was his life mate. He proposed—and was accepted—in a romantic setting, among the Japanese cherry trees that rim Washington's Tidal Basin. They did not, however, marry immediately. Long engagements were the custom then, and in any event Sam's salary was inadequate for raising a family.

In his off-work hours, Sam kept up his athletic activities, principally basketball, which he played with a team known as the Washington Yankees. The Yankee club was a semi-pro aggregation, which charged an admission fee for some of its games and paid the players a small stipend. Sam Solomon, however, never accepted a nickel; basketball, he felt, was something one did for the fun of it and taking money would diminish the enjoyment.

It was with the Yankees, in 1922, that Sam made another acquaintance who was to play a large part in his future life, an Army officer and nationally famous West Point athlete named Eugene Vidal. In one of the Yankees' games, against the Alexandria Dreadnoughts, Vidal made a guest-star appearance with the Virginia team. It was a rough, hotly-contested game and at one critical point Sam and Gene Vidal dove simultaneously for a loose ball. Vidal's knee collided with Solomon's jaw and Sam dropped to the boards, unconscious. Several years later, when the two renewed their acquaintance, Vidal remarked,

"I remember you—from the Washington Yankees."

"I've never forgotten you," Sam replied, rubbing his jaw.

It was not long after the Yankee-Dreadnought clash that Sam dropped out of basketball, but it was not the knockout that brought about his decision. George Preston Marshall, the Washington laundry owner who was later to found the Washington Redskins of the National Football League, took over the semi-pro Yankees. In return for his financial support, Marshall insisted that the players wear jerseys with "PALACE LAUNDRY" inscribed in large lettering. That offended the Solomon sense of propriety. It was not the commercialism that bothered him; in fact, Sam found it difficult to explain to himself exactly why he could not accept the laundry identification. It was just something that Sam Solomon did not do. So he resigned from the team and found another outlet for his sports enthusiasm, as unpaid assistant athletic director of Washington's Unitarian Church.

In 1920 Sam's father died and Sam became the primary support of his brother and sisters. Money—or more properly the lack of it—became a real problem. At Treasury, Sam had shown a ready aptitude for loan accounting and had moved up the ladder. After little more than a year on the job, he had been promoted to section chief in charge of almost a hundred people. But even with the salary increase the promotion had brought, Sam was making barely thirty dollars a week at the time of his father's death.

For months he brooded about his financial situation and what to do about it. Then, one day in 1923, he totaled up his checking account balance and found he had exactly one dollar and eighty cents. If that was all he could show after four years at Treasury, Sam reasoned, he would probably not be much better off in another four years. He was going nowhere. He made an instant decision to leave the Treasury and explore more promising fields, although he was not quite sure where to look for them.

Informed of this decision, C. N. McGroarty, Sam's boss at the Treasury Department, was astounded. McGroarty was himself a career Federal employee and in his experience people did not just walk away from the lifetime security of a government job.

"Solomon," McGroarty asked, "are you aware that you could remain here all your working life?"

Sam nodded.

"That's exactly what I'm afraid of," he replied, and he stuck to his decision despite McGroarty's advice to remain.

Sam found an interim career in real estate. With Ludo Pickett, another former Treasury employee who had made a similar decision, he formed Realty Investment Corporation, dealing in the sale of homes and business properties. After two years, the partnership was dissolved and each continued independently in the same type of business. In real estate, Sam made more money than he had at the Treasury, but hardly enough to be considered prosperous.

On December 26, 1923, after an engagement of almost five years, Sam and Alma Garber were married. The ceremony, conducted by the minister of Alma's Primitive Baptist Church, was held in the parlor of Alma's home, filled to overflowing with friends and relatives. The newlyweds took a brief honeymoon in Florida, traveling one way by train and returning by ship. Back in Washington, they moved into a "flat" in a two-family house on Harvard Street, not far from Alma's family home.

In three years of real estate work, Sam enjoyed sporadic success, but he did not feel that he had yet found his real niche in business. He decided to try another tack—building and selling his own homes—undeterred by the fact that he had accumulated very little capital. He teamed with Jimmy Latta, a friend from Central High days and the son of a White House aide. Latta, an engineer, knew something about building homes and Sam had developed a considerable expertise in matters of sales and finance. With minimal cash investment, the partners were able to obtain first and second trust loans to cover the purchase of land and the start of construction. They acquired 40 lots in a desirable area of Northwest Washington along and adjacent to 16th Street, one of the city's main thoroughfares, and over the next two years they built 24 homes.

In the meantime, the Solomons had moved several times as the family expanded. Sister Mildred was living with the Solomons. Sam and Alma's firstborn, a son they named Robert, arrived in 1926 and a second son, Richard, followed a year and a half later. So in 1928, looking for roomier quarters, the Solomons bought a home of their own, a frame house with more than an acre of land in Silver Spring,

Maryland. The new house, later expanded, was to be the family home from that time on. Silver Spring, in the years that followed, was to grow from a sparsely-populated countryside setting into a sprawling suburb of Washington, until the once-isolated Solomon home was completely surrounded by new construction.

In 1928, Sam's home building business was flagging. Some of the original 16 houses had been sold but the others found no takers; eight additional houses started later were in various stages of completion. Solomon and Latta were finding it increasingly difficult to meet their loan payments.

In an effort to resolve the dilemma with a quick financial coup, Sam took a gamble. He acquired title to two partially-finished buildings on Capitol Hill within a stone's throw of the Capitol itself. Sam planned to complete the buildings and lease them to the government of the District of Columbia, which had a plan afoot to convert the properties into a District detention home and clinic.

For a while it looked as though Sam had made a great move; District officials went so far as to execute a memorandum of intent to lease the buildings. Then the Solomon luck ran out. Word leaked to the newspapers and the story of the detention home plan was bannered on the front pages. There was a tremendous uproar from Washington's citizenry, outraged at the idea of a jailhouse adjoining the Capitol grounds. The District's embarrassed officialdom beat a hasty retreat. They dropped the conversion proposal, reneged on their commitment and Sam Solomon became the unhappy owner of two unfinished buildings he could not sell and could not otherwise pay for.

The collapse of the detention home deal tolled the end of Sam's building venture. He owed more than $70,000 and much as he detested the idea, there was only one way in which he could extricate himself from the financial morass; he was forced to file bankruptcy proceedings. Legally, bankruptcy cleared him of debt, but Sam's pride and honesty would not permit him to accept that aspect of the bankruptcy law. He wanted respite, not absolution, and he wrote each of his creditors to that effect. It may take a while, he told them, but you will get every penny owed you. It did take a while, a good many years, but Sam whittled away at his mountain of debts until eventually there were no more.

A disheartened Sam Solomon went back to selling real estate and continued in that activity, again with intermittent success, for several years thereafter. It was during this unexciting and not overly remunerative period, in 1931, that there came the chance encounter that was to redirect the course of Sam's career and plunge him into the fascinating world of aviation, the pursuit which he had long considered but never actively sought.

By this time, Sam had acquired a considerable reputation in Washington circles. He was known as an extremely honest person and one whose veracity was beyond question. He lived by an axiom learned years earlier from his parents: "Always tell the truth, then you won't have to remember what you said." And, although truth and honesty are traits more often associated with naivete than with shrewdness, Sam was nonetheless a clever and imaginative businessman who frequently came up with angles that escaped others.

The Solomon reputation prompted a friend—a World War I naval aviator named Harry Harris—to contact Sam and ask his assistance. A group of six investors, Harris related, had pooled resources to build and operate a public swimming pool on the grounds of Washington-Hoover Airport. The group's collective expertise in swimming pool operation amounted to practically nothing. They had got in over their heads, Harris told Sam, and they needed help to bail them out of a troublesome situation. Could Sam spare the time to look into their problem?

The memory of his own bankruptcy still fresh, Sam was sympathetic to anyone in financial straits. He agreed to look into the matter and Harris arranged a meeting.

Best known of the swimming pool investors was Amelia Earhart Putnam, a tall, tousle-headed woman with a magnificent smile and a grand sense of humor. Then in her early thirties, Amelia had more than a decade of flying experience and already ranked as America's foremost aviatrix. In 1928, a year after Charles Lindbergh had made the first solo flight across the Atlantic, Amelia Earhart had made headlines as the first woman to fly the ocean; she had not, on that flight, piloted the airplane, but had flown as a passenger in a Fokker trimotor commanded by Wilmer Stultz. Later, flying her own Lockheed Vega, Amelia set a number of inter-city speed records in the United States, then capped her career by becoming the first woman to fly solo across the Atlantic. A year before Sam Solomon's first meeting with Amelia, she had married author, publisher and explorer George Palmer Putnam.

Among Amelia's partners were Paul F. Collins and Eugene Vidal, the same Vidal whose knee had knocked Sam galley-west in the Yankee-Dreadnought basketball game a decade earlier.

Paul Collins had been a pilot in World War I and had found postwar employment in one of the most hazardous flight ventures of all time: the experiment conducted by the U.S. Postal Service in flying mail around the clock in fair or foul weather. Of the first 40 pilots hired for that service, 31 were killed in crashes. Collins himself had had a close call, bailing out of a crippled plane. After leaving the airmail service, he had joined Transcontinental Air Transport, the predecessor of Trans World Airlines, and had become TAT's general superintendent.

It was at TAT that Collins met Gene Vidal, who was the line's assistant general manager. A polished, sophisticated man, Vidal was a pilot himself, but at TAT his work involved sales, advertising and public relations rather than the operational end of the business.

In 1930, Collins and Vidal had teamed to start a new airline financed by the Ludington brothers of Philadelphia, Collins as vice president-operations and Vidal as general manager. Called Ludington Lines the airline operated briefly between Washington, Philadelphia and New York. But, in those early days of air transport, it was next to impossible to survive on passenger fares; an airline needed a government airmail contract to survive. Twice Ludington bid for airmail routes and twice lost out. The second turndown spelled the demise of Ludington Lines. The Ludington brothers decided to sell out to Eastern Air Transport, later Eastern Air Lines, a much larger competitor operating in the same areas. It was during Ludington Lines' decline that Collins and Vidal had joined Amelia and three others in the swimming pool venture.

In their office in the swimming pool administration building adjacent to the pool itself, Sam met with the investors and they outlined their difficulties. They had decided initially on a saltwater pool, unaware of the tremendous amount of salt—and the cost of it—needed for the seawater effect they sought. They had first used well water, but it was too cold for comfort, necessitating an expensive conversion to city water. Then the tons of salt started to corrode the pipes and valves. And, of course, Washington's rarely-stable weather influenced patronage; a few cold or rainy weekends, particularly holiday weekends, could ruin a season. With fluctuating patronage and expenses greater than anticipated, the pool operators were losing more money than they could afford and they had gone heavily into debt. In short, they wanted out.

To Sam Solomon the problem was not a particularly taxing one. The pool was being operated under a lease from National Aviation Corporation, an aviation investment firm which owned the airport property. Sam went to New York and talked with Frank Russell, vice president of the corporation. Sam argued that, properly managed, the pool could be a profitable operation and he persuaded Russell to buy back the lease for $35,000, with the understanding that the money would be used to pay off all creditors. Thus, the investors escaped from the pool business with little damage to their purses and Sam won their warm gratitude.

It was on his visit to New York to see Russell that Sam made his first airplane flight, in a Fleetstar monoplane, a small passenger craft of the day. It was an interesting experience, Sam felt, though not a particularly exciting one. It seemed to him that the cab ride from Newark Airport to Manhattan, at racetrack pace across the Jersey marshes on a bumpy, winding road, was far more dangerous.

From the swimming pool extrication emerged a fast friendship between Sam, Amelia, Collins and Vidal. They met frequently, at ping-pong sessions in the pool building, in Manhattan, or at Amelia's palatial home in Rye, New York. Often their discussions focused on "What shall we do?" All four were looking for a new business venture, hopefully one that was interesting and profitable and would permit them to pool their talents.

In 1932, a year which witnessed the birth of the Solomons' third son, William, Sam engaged in his first cooperative enterprise with his new friends. Late in that year, just after Franklin D. Roosevelt's election to the Presidency, Collins, Vidal and Sam had a get-together in New York. Vidal, who frequently visited Manhattan and invariably stayed at the New Yorker Hotel, had received a letter from the hotel's president. Because of the frequency of Gene's visits, the letter advised, the hotel was awarding him a bonus—free use of a suite for as long as he desired. Vidal immediately contacted Collins and Solomon and invited them to share his bonanza.

Lounging in the luxurious suite, they started a "What shall we do?" discussion.

"How about silver?" Vidal asked.

His father-in-law, Vidal explained, had told him that anyone could make money by investing in silver. Gene's father-in-law was Thomas Gore, the blind U.S. Senator from Oklahoma, and when Senator Gore said anything, people listened.

"How do you go about it?" Sam asked. Vidal had no idea, so Sam got on the phone to Frank Russell, of National Aviation Corporation. Russell, it turned out, wasn't sure either, but he said he would check and call back. He did.

"You buy something called a silver future," he reported.

Sam Solomon, speaking for the impromptu partnership allowed that he hadn't the faintest idea what that was, but it sounded all right and what was the least amount of money they could invest?

"You'll need a minimum of one thousand," said Russell. "Have you guys got a thousand?" Sam cupped his hand over the phone and asked Collins and Vidal in turn if they had three hundred thirty-three dollars. They said yes. Sam asked himself the same question and decided that, although he was not overloaded with cash, he could manage.

"We've got it," he told Russell. "Buy us one."

Back in Washington, the trio learned a little more about their investment. The thousand dollars represented a deposit against the purchase of ten thousand ounces of silver on margin. They were somewhat nervous; it sounded like an awful lot of silver. Every day they checked the Washington papers for a line on the silver market, but never found a word. They interrupted their ping-pong sessions frequently to call the brokerage house and ask the price of silver. After several days of "sweating it out," the partners decided that their future lay in something less nebulous than silver futures and Sam was delegated to advise the brokerage firm that they wanted to sell.

"We say the hell with it," Sam told the brokerage man. "If the price of silver isn't important enough to be in the Washington papers, it isn't important enough for us to hold."

The trio came out of the bold venture with a small profit, a few hundred dollars. It wasn't much, but it served as the cornerstone of a far greater endeavor; soon thereafter the money was used to cover the initial expense of incorporating what was one day to become a major American airline.

CHAPTER III
Birth of an Airline

In the five years prior to The Great Silver Futures Coup, events were transpiring in New England that were later to have marked impact on the lives of Sam Solomon, Amelia Earhart, Gene Vidal and Paul Collins, although none of them was involved in the initial developments.

In 1927, George Hannauer and Gerrit Fort, president and vice president respectively of the Boston and Maine Railroad, began to think seriously of broadening their operations to include air transportation. The Boston and Maine had already entered the passenger bus business and Hannauer and Fort now proposed that the company take a further step to provide coordinated rail, highway and air services. There was a qualification to the proposal: "As soon as air transportation becomes economical."

Fort was assigned the task of studying the economics of air transportation. Heading a special research committee, he investigated passenger and air mail potential and reluctantly concluded that the day of the commercial airplane had not yet arrived. The Boston and Maine total transportation concept lay dormant.

In 1930, Edward S. French became president of the Boston and Maine and named as his assistant Laurence S. Whittemore. The visionary Whittemore, although a career railroader, was an aviation enthusiast and a firm believer in the future of air transportation. He prophesied that the time was fast approaching when railroaders "would look up and see the business that had formerly been on the railroad track."

Whittemore picked up the total transportation idea where Fort had left off and sought to convince French that the concept was sound. He was abetted in his efforts by one significant development. About the time French ascended to the presidency of the railroad, Congress authorized a new type of airmail payment. Formerly, airlines were paid only for the mail they carried and it was rarely enough to get excited about. Under the new authorization, the Postmaster General would pay a flat rate for each plane-mile flown, regardless of the volume of airmail as long as there was *some* airmail. This, Whittemore felt, would make a world of difference in airline economics. He argued that airline service in New England was inevitable and that the Boston and Maine would be far better off if it could control the advent. French, initially skeptical, was finally won over by Whittemore's boundless enthusiasm and the Boston and Maine decided to go into the aviation business.

In determining air routes, the Boston and Maine's survey group proposed a network between Boston and Bangor, Maine, with intermediate stops at Portland and other Maine cities. Such service would conflict with the rail routes of another line, the Maine Central Railroad, a company closely connected with the Boston and Maine through interlocking directorships. If the service was to be initiated, Maine Central would have to be a part of it. So Whittemore began another selling job, this time on Morris McDonald, president of the Maine Central. McDonald at first stated flatly that it was a crazy idea, but eventually he succumbed to Whittemore's persuasion as had French, with the understanding that the Boston and Maine would carry the primary responsibility.

The next task was to contract with an airline. There was one obvious choice—Pan American Airways, founded and headed by Juan Terry Trippe. Pan Am, operating Sikorsky flying boats, was pioneering long-distance overwater travel from Florida to the Caribbean islands, Central and South America. It had sound management, a good financial position and an impressive safety record. Of greater importance, Pan Am was already interested in operations north of Boston and had undertaken an independent survey of weather conditions, passenger volume and facilities between Boston and Halifax, Nova Scotia. Juan Trippe's interest in the Northeast differed from that of the Boston and Maine. Trippe, constantly seeking expansion, was looking toward the possibility of flying the North Atlantic to England, using Halifax as the jumping-off point. He was not particularly interested in domestic operations but felt that the Boston-Bangor-Halifax run would provide a foundation for transatlantic service.

French and Whittemore approached Trippe and the three concluded an arrangement whereby the railroads would provide financial backing and Pan Am would handle the operational end of the partnership. It was agreed that the initial service would be confined to the summer months because of the seasonal nature of travel in New England. The Pan Am/railroads partnership was to apply only to the Boston-Bangor run and the intermediate points; Pan Am would operate independently on the Bangor-Halifax segment of the route.

On August 1, 1931, the first scheduled air service in northern New England was launched. Pan Am flew 12-passenger Fokker trimotors on the New England segments and Sikorsky S-41B's of similar capacity on the Halifax run. In a two-month season, the airline carried more than 2,000 passengers, and although the service produced a net loss of $14,000 the railroads were eminently satisfied. It was felt that a longer season, from June through October, coupled with the higher capacity airplanes that Trippe proposed to operate, would bring about a highly profitable operation in the following year.

In 1932, however, Trippe decided not to renew his contract with the railroads. He had been unable to acquire landing rights in England because the British would agree to such a deal only if they were granted reciprocal rights to fly the Atlantic to the United States and Britain's Imperial Airways was not yet ready for transoceanic flight. His dream of a transatlantic route temporarily shelved, Trippe had no further interest in New England/Canada service.

Disappointed, Laurence Whittemore looked elsewhere for an airline operator. He had heard of the fine work accomplished by Paul Collins and Gene Vidal as operators of Ludington Lines, so he contacted Vidal with a proposal similar to that offered Pan Am: the railroads would subsidize the service to some extent, but the operators would have to provide the airplanes and their crews and maintain the equipment. Vidal discussed it with the Ludingtons, who were not interested, and then with Collins. It was an attractive proposition but, even pooling their resources, Vidal and Collins did not have the kind of money that would be needed. With the nation still in the throes of its greatest depression, they felt it would be next to impossible to find outside financing. Reluctantly, Vidal called Whittemore and declined. The Boston and Maine decided to abandon the air service for 1932 and, hopefully, to revive it in 1933 if an acceptable operator could be found.

* * * * * * * *

In the summer of 1933, the foursome of Sam Solomon, Amelia Earhart Putnam, Paul Collins and Gene Vidal held one of their get-togethers at the Putnam home in Rye, New York. Sitting on the living room floor, because Amelia liked the informality and "coziness" of floor-sitting, they engaged in a "What shall we do?" discussion. It was Amelia who voiced the most interesting proposal.

"Let's start an airline."

Collins and Vidal immediately concurred. Vidal recalled his talk with Whittemore of the Boston and Maine and suggested that that opportunity might still be open. But Sam demurred.

"You three are aviators," he said, "but I don't know a thing about airplanes and anyway I'm scared of them."

His friends mounted a strong argument. Among them, they said, they certainly had the know-how for the operational end of running an airline, but what they needed to solidify the team was a competent businessman and everyone knew Sam Solomon was one of the best. Sam wavered but continued to hold out.

"Well," said Amelia, as if reluctantly shelving the airline notion, "whatever we do, let's do it together." That turned Sam Solomon around. He didn't want to be the veto vote on a proposal that obviously excited the others. He very much wanted to team with this group of wonderful people and if they wanted an airline, well, why not?

"All right, count me in," he said, somewhat surprised at his quick reversal. "I want to be a vice president," he added. "When I was a kid, growing up, I read every one of the Horatio Alger books and I always wanted to become a railroad president. But to do that—at least Alger's way—you have to start as a brakeman. It's a little late for that. I don't suppose I can be president of an airline, either, but at least I can be a vice president."

The decision triggered some rapid action. Using the small profit from the silver venture to cover legal expenses, the group formed National Airways Corporation, incorporated in the State of Delaware. Each of the four put up $2500 for an initial working capital of $10,000. Collins, senior from the standpoint of operational experience, was named president. Amelia became first vice president, Sam second. Vidal, however, was to play no active part in National Airways' operations. While the preparatory work was under way, he had been offered a government post as director of the Bureau of Air Commerce. It was an important job involving the development of regulations for a rapidly-expanding American aviation system and Gene could not turn it down.

Before he bowed out of active participation, however, Vidal contacted Laurence Whittemore to find out if the Boston and Maine was still looking for an operator. It was.

Sam Solomon was delegated to be National Airways' contract negotiator. In meetings with Boston and Maine officials, he worked out an arrangement whereby National Airways would furnish the airplanes and their pilots and take responsibility for the conduct of flight operations; the railroads—Maine Central again a participant—would guarantee a certain number of passengers, handle ticket sales through their own outlets and provide communications and publicity. The railroads laid down the initial routes, to stations where they felt they could best develop passenger volume: Boston-Portland-Bangor, with alternate routings through Waterville and Rockland, Maine.

The next step was to make an operational entity of National Airways, which was still a paper corporation. There were three basic essentials: money, airplanes, and people to fly and maintain them.

As for the money, Collins and Solomon felt they could get by on the original capitalization of ten thousand dollars, by buying used aircraft and arranging lines of credit wherever possible. But even at 1933 prices, it took extraordinary optimism to start an airline with so thin an exchequer. It had taken several million dollars to launch one of the major airlines of that period and even little Ludington Lines had been backed to the extent of a quarter of a million. To say that National Airways started life on a shoestring would be overstatement; it was more like a broken shoestring.

The acquisition of airplanes, which should have been the major problem with so little cash in hand, proved to be a simple matter because Paul Collins knew exactly where to go for them. The demise of Ludington, which Collins had mourned a short time earlier, now turned out to be National Airways' salvation.

In purchasing Ludington, Eastern Air Transport had acquired the smaller line's fleet of six Stinson trimotors, which had only 10 seats, five on either side of a narrow aisle. Eastern, rapidly emerging as the air transport giant of the East Coast, was flying bigger and faster equipment and had no use for the Stinsons. The trimotors, though small for commercial operations, were too big and too costly to operate to attract private buyers. So Collins, who had paid $22,500 each for the Stinsons only three years earlier, brazenly offered $2,-500 apiece for two planes and was not too surprised when Captain Thomas Doe, president of Eastern, accepted. Doe, happy to be rid of the unwanted aircraft, even threw in a generous supply of spare parts. It was a great bargain in the opinion of all the partners except Gene Vidal, who thought Collins had offered too much.

It was agreed that Eastern would turn over the airplanes on August 7 and, to the amazement of the railroad people, Collins and Solomon announced they would start airline service on August 11, less than a month after the start of negotiations.

Thus,.National Airways had a "fleet" at a real bargain price and there were other advantages in buying the Stinsons. Having operated them at Ludington, Collins was thoroughly familiar with their flight characteristics and their operating and maintenance costs. There was another bonus: although more modern airliners required a pilot and co-pilot, the Stinson had been designed for single-pilot operation, which substantially reduced payroll costs.

The next step was to hire people. With the service inaugural date coming up fast, Collins didn't have much time, but here again he benefited from the collapse of Ludington Lines. Most of the Ludington personnel had been absorbed by Eastern Air Transport, but many of them were not especially happy at Eastern; they had lost seniority in the transfer. Collins set his sights on those he felt might be looking for greener pastures and, settling himself at a telephone, he began a two-day round of calls.

His primary need was a chief pilot and Collins had the man in mind: Milton H. Anderson, still a young man but a thoroughly experienced pilot who had been with Collins both at Ludington and at Transcontinental Air Transport. A line captain at Ludington, Anderson had been demoted to co-pilot in the switch to Eastern. He leaped at the chance to get a plane command again, or more properly a two-plane command.

Collins had decided that a four-pilot crew, with himself in reserve, would suffice. He lined up two more of the Ludington people, Earl Smith and Earle Steele. For the fourth pilot, Collins wanted a man who had flight experience in New England and was familiar with the terrain and the reputedly-terrible weather conditions; he found one in Hazen Bean, who had been flying for a small company operating between Boston and Albany.

The other major personnel requirement was a chief of maintenance. Once again Collins dipped into the Ludington pool and came up with Clarence M. Belinn. Belinn was ready for a new job, although somewhat taken aback when he was told he had two days to hire a crew and report with them to Washington. Belinn took a page from the Collins book and hired two master mechanics who had served with Ludington.

One job remained—finding hangar space. This proved tougher than anticipated; there was no space available at Boston. Collins finally found a ramshackle, unheated hangar at the Portland terminus, so Portland, rather than Boston, became the interim operations center for the airline. It was also decided, about this time, that the line would formally be known as Boston-Maine Airways; National Airways would remain in existence, but only as a contractual entity, the airline's operational designation.

On August 7, 1933, Sam Solomon and Paul Collins took delivery of their two Stinson trimotors at Washington-Hoover Airport. It was a proud moment; practically all of the airline's personnel was on hand and to them the two little Stinsons looked like giant liners of the sky. The planes were loaded with all of the airline's possessions: the spare parts Eastern had thrown into the bargain, a single reserve

Officials of Boston-Maine Airways, forerunner of Northeast Airlines, pose beside their trimotor Stinson on the occasion of the airline's first flight. Left to right: W. O. Wright, general passenger traffic manager of the Boston and Maine Railroad; Arthur B. Nichols, vice president of the railroad; Sam Solomon; Amelia Earhart; Laurence F. Whittemore; and Paul Collins.

engine and a lone file cabinet. Anderson took the controls of one airplane, Earle Steele the other, and the two Stinsons departed from Boston. Sam Solomon stayed behind; he had business in Washington, but he was to follow the group the next day.

On August 8, while Sam and Alma Solomon were en route to Boston, Collins loaded all his pilots into the two Stinsons and conducted a proving flight over the network. Since most of the group had never flown in New England, this was a necessary preliminary to check out weather conditions and to explore the fields into which Boston-Maine Airways would be flying.

The following day, August 9, marked the final preparatory step, a dress rehearsal designed to publicize the upcoming inauguration of regular passenger service. At Boston in sunny, cloudless weather, 10 passengers boarded the Stinson: Sam and Alma Solomon; Paul Collins; Amelia Earhart Putnam; Laurence Whittemore; Arthur B. Nichols, vice president of the Boston and Maine Railroad; W. O. Wright, general passenger traffic manager of the Boston and Maine; and three reporters from the Boston newspapers.

With Milton Anderson at the controls of the Stinson, the group flew to Portland, then to Rockland, Bangor and Waterville. At each city, crowds ranging from several hundred to more than a thousand people gathered, mostly to see Amelia. There were brief ceremonies at each stop, highlighted by Amelia's remarks on the wonders of flight and the advantages of air travel. At Rockland, Amelia was introduced by Mayor Charles M. Richardson, who talked in glowing terms of the world renowned aviatrix—then forgot her name! Not the least offended, Amelia joined in the roar of laughter.

Sam Solomon missed most of the preview flight. He remained behind in Portland, to arrange credit with the local Texaco office for fuel for the return flight, a necessity typical of the money-short atmosphere in which the airline was to operate for a long time thereafter.

August 11, 1933, was a banner day for Boston-Maine Airways, the formal start of the airline's commercial service. Less than two months had elapsed since the four partners had met at Amelia's home and launched a dream. The railroad officials had been skeptical that an airline, even a small one, could be created from scratch and ready for duty in such a brief span. But there it was. On the ramp at Logan Airport sat one of the Stinsons, which, piloted by Hazen Bean, would take the first payload north to Portland and Bangor. At Portland, Milton Anderson was readying the other trimotor for a southbound flight to Boston.

On board Bean's inaugural flight were Amelia Earhart Putnam

and Gene Vidal, the latter in his new capacity as director of the Bureau of Air Commerce. The other eight seats were filled by the airline's first passengers, who had paid $5.60 for a one-way flight to Portland or $12.60 for the longer run to Bangor. The 96-mile trip to Portland went smoothly. Bean discharged some passengers, boarded others and took off for Bangor. Anderson, after a slight weather delay, took off from Portland with four Boston-bound passengers. Boston-Maine Airways was officially in business.

****

After the inaugural flights, Boston-Maine Airways settled into what might be termed "hectic routine." Money was the major problem; for a long time after inaugural day, a full passenger load was a rarity and frequently a plane took off with zero payload. There was no airmail subsidy; concentrating on developing airmail service between the nation's largest metropolitan areas, the Post Office Department was not letting contracts for service north of Boston. Railroad funding permitted Collins and Solomon to meet the payroll, but there were no profits.

Each of the three partners assumed a specific area of responsibility. It was Paul Collins' job, with the help of Clarence Belinn, to keep the planes in the air and meet schedules. This was difficult from the start but it became doubly so with the decision to continue regular service throughout the winter months. Frequent fog, heavy snows, strong winds and rough air combined to plague the fledgling airline. Navigation was a problem; the Stinsons had no radios, but that was academic because there were no radio ground stations along the routes being flown.

The prime enemy was the bitter New England cold, with temperatures at times dipping to 25 degrees below zero. Working in their unheated hangar, Belinn and his crew lived through an agonizing winter, each night desperately trying to keep the engines warm enough so they would start in the morning. They stuffed newspapers into the engine exhaust stacks to block out moisture and prevent freezing, then blanketed the whole mounting with engine covers. Each night they drained the oil and stored it in the heated office; even so, the oil frequently had to be pre-heated in the morning before it could be poured back into the engine.

The heavy snows of the area posed an additional problem. After each snowfall, a runway strip had to be plowed. The airport ranked at the bottom of the plowing priority list, as far as the municipalities being served were concerned. They did handle some of the plowing, after the city streets were cleared, but Collins had to hire commercial plows a good part of the time.

Taking off in the snow with wheeled gear was another problem. Collins could have used skis on the trimotors, but then the planes would not have been able to land at Boston, where the runways were usually clear. Belinn solved that dilemma by buying truck chains and welding additional links to them to get proper traction for the Stinsons' wheels.

Amelia took on the sales and public relations job. In the early thirties, resistance to air travel was monumental. To the average person, flight was something like tightrope walking—it was an interesting spectacle to watch but far too dangerous a pastime for sensible people. Sam, Collins, Amelia and Herbert Baldwin, a publicity man provided by the railroads, visited every city on the Boston-Maine Airways network, talking up the convenience of air travel and its safety. They contacted community leaders and appeared before civic clubs, where there was always a crowd, attracted by the opportunity to meet America's leading aviatrix.

On Saturdays, when the airline operated on a reduced schedule and one of the airplanes was available, the sales promotion team would visit one of the cities and offer free, 10-minute sight-seeing trips. Initially, there were few takers; the plane was rarely filled. Amelia switched tactics and focused on women's groups, on the theory that if she could convince the wives, the husbands would follow. The women proved more airminded than the men and the demonstration flights became more and more popular. Once, the Bangor Chamber of Commerce held a Women's Day, with Amelia as guest of honor and free rides for as many women as could be accommodated. Ten thousand people turned out and more than 200 women, two of them nonagenarians, made brief flights. It was an exhausting promotional program, but it began to pay dividends; there was no immediate barrage of ticket sales, but gradually the airline's passenger load factor edged upward.

For Sam Solomon, the first winter in New England was a particularly hectic period. Sam had accepted a new job in Washington, so he had, in effect, two full-time jobs in locales more than 400 miles apart.[1]

[1] When Sam Solomon accepted the job of running his home-town airport, he had no intention of leaving the airline; he was by now thoroughly immersed in the airline project and exhilarated by the challenge it presented. He decided that somehow he could handle the dual assignment of airport manager in Washington and airline executive in Boston. Although today it seems a near impossibility, he managed it. How he did so is detailed later. However, Solomon's tendency to accept multiple assignments running concurrently—at one time he had three major jobs—poses a problem for orderly continuity; a strictly chronological narrative would bog down in confusion. For that reason, this book is chapterized to cover one-at-a-time each of Solomon's dissimilar endeavors.

In his airline capacity, Sam had a number of jobs. As businessman member of the management trio, he supervised general administration and finance. Additionally, he served as the airline's liaison with its railroad backers. Sam had an excellent relationship with Laurence Whittemore, who continued to represent the railroad group; they agreed that whenever a difficulty arose, they would settle it between them, without the help of joint committees which tended to escalate minor difficulties into major problems. The system worked well; there were frequent conflicts but they were invariably and quickly resolved in quiet discussion between the two.

Sam also acted as contact man with the communities served by the airline. One of his tasks was to get the municipalities to improve their facilities. The airfields being used were initially nothing more than cow-pastures or hayfields owned by local farmers who leased landing rights to the airline. Collins' pilots somehow managed to get into and out of these postage-stamp airports, but they were patently inadequate for safe and efficient operations. There was a need for clearing land to extend and widen the runways, and perhaps for a waiting room, communications and other ground facilities.

Airline service was still not important enough to interest the communities in spending municipal money on airport development. Sam Solomon, however, found a way. Under President Roosevelt's Works Progress Administration program, it was possible to get Federal funding for improvements to municipally-owned airports. The fields into which Boston-Maine Airways was operating were, for the most part, privately owned, but Sam was instrumental in getting the owners to deed a small portion of their properties—the landing strip, for example—to the cities or towns. In this manner, the private owner retained most of his property and continued to receive landing fees from the airline, but since a part of the airfield complex was municipally owned the airport qualified for government aid.

Solomon devoted the major portion of his energies to route expansion. Although an aviation tyro, he had recognized from the start that consistent growth of the airline depended upon broadening the network, to expand the customer-potential base by making the service available to the greatest possible number of people. Therefore, he sought as much route expansion as the line's two airplanes—bolstered by purchase of a third Stinson in 1934—could handle. Expansion involved first, the approval of the Bureau of Air Commerce, fortunately headed by Gene Vidal, and second, the negotiation of landing rights with the municipality.

As soon as the airline consolidated operations on its northeasterly route—Boston to Bangor—Boston-Maine Airways created a northwesterly route running from Boston through Concord, New Hampshire, to White River Junction, Montpelier-Barre and Burlington, all in Vermont. In accord with the policy of coordinating with the railroads whose trackage was being overflown, this extension involved the acquisition of another partner, the Central Vermont Railroad. The official corporate name became the Boston-Maine, Maine Central and Central Vermont Airways. This was too much to paint on the fuselages of the little Stinsons, so to the public eye the airline remained the Boston-Maine Airways.

Other route additions followed. The northeasterly route was extended to Caribou at the northern tip of Maine near the Canadian border, with additional intermediate stops at Augusta and Bar Harbor, Maine. The northwesterly route was pushed across the Canadian border to Montreal, making the Boston-Maine an international airline.

Although the participants later wondered how, the airline survived its first, brutal winter without an accident, and in the spring of 1934 Collins finally was able to acquire hangar space—with heat—at Boston's Logan Airport. This was not only a heaven-sent boon to Belinn's frostbitten maintenance crew, it also allowed centralization of the operations and administrative functions in one locale.

In that same year came another major development. Earlier, in the wake of an investigation of irregularities in the award of airmail contracts, President Roosevelt had cancelled airline participation and directed the Army to fly the mail. It was not the wisest decision he ever made. Ill-equipped and inexperienced in bad-weather flight, Army pilots met with one fatal crash after another until public opinion clamored for a return to airline mail-haulage. In May, 1934, the President ordered the Postmaster General to accept bids from the airlines. Boston-Maine Airways bid for and won the contract for mail service north of Boston.

Under the contract, the airline received a payment for each bag of mail it carried, even if the bag held only one letter. Airmail, however, was not yet popular in New England and all too often the mail bag was empty. This problem was readily solved. The airline's station managers at each end of the route took to writing each other a daily letter and putting an airmail stamp on it. This assured that there would be a mail payment for every day. The airmail subsidy was hardly sufficient to bring the airline overnight prosperity, but it did take the load off the railroad backers, who might otherwise have had some second thoughts about their air transportation venture.

Looking toward further expansion of the route system, Sam began to think in grand terms: How about hitting the larger cities? What about extending the system south to New York and Washington, west to Chicago? This, of course, would take an enormous amount of money for additional airplanes, new facilities and all the other expenses attendant upon opening new routes. The railroads could not be expected to go along with the idea; they were interested only in their own locales, and in any event they probably could not muster the type of backing that would be required. The expansion would have to come in the form of a separate operating entity backed by new financing. Sam and Paul Collins started looking for a new money source.

One day Collins reported to Sam that he had made contact with a potential backer, a multimillionaire named Sam Rosoff. Rosoff, who had ambitions of becoming an airline boss, wanted them to come to New York immediately to talk about route expansion. Sam telephoned Amelia's husband, George Putnam, and asked him to find out all he could about Rosoff. Putnam reported that there was no question about Rosoff's financial position; a man of fantastic ability, he had made a fortune building subways and had then branched out into a broad network of commercial avenues.

In New York, Solomon and Collins met Rosoff and his mild-mannered associate at a club that still had all the trappings of the speakeasy it had been until a year earlier, when the nation's prohibition law had been repealed. Rosoff was a little, gnome-like man. His colossal ego, however, made up for his lack of stature. He was loud and overbearing, and typical of his attitude toward people was his introduction of his associate:

"This is my partner, Bulova, he makes watches." Arde Bulova, who had little to say while Rosoff was on stage, was himself a nationally-known and highly-respected figure, manufacturer of a line of quality watches and clocks.

Over drinks, Rosoff held forth at length on his favorite subject—Sam Rosoff—and sought to impress them with his importance by reciting a litany of his multiple business ventures. "Right now, I'm on a brewery binge," he said. "I just bought the King's brewery and I'm about to buy another one." He added: "I got no brains but I got the money to buy them."

Rosoff took his guests to an expensive restaurant, where he made an entrance like Caesar returning from Gaul, loudly greeting by name the maitre d'hotel, the waiters and many of the customers. He demanded one waiter for each of his party and dispensed with the business of food-selection by pointing his finger at each in turn and saying, "You'll have a steak." Sam and Paul Collins exchanged glances. Was this the kind of partner they wanted?

After dinner, the group repaired to Rosoff's apartment and got down to business. Sam outlined the route extensions he had in mind and what was involved in the way of money. The airplanes, he said, could be obtained cheaply, they had an option on some used Stinsons no longer needed by American Airlines.

Rosoff snorted. There would be no used airplanes on *his* airline. What about new ones?

Well, Collins related, Lockheed Aircraft had developed a fine new small airliner called the Electra, but it was selling for $50,000. Rosoff became more interested. He wanted to know more about the plane and its builder. Was it a good "factory" and where was it located? Collins told him.

"Bulova," said Rosoff, turning to his partner, "get out to California and buy that factory."

Rosoff wound up the interview by saying that he was interested in the proposal and that Bulova would be in touch with them. But, in a post-meeting critique, Sam and Collins decided that their airline would never be the same with Rosoff in the driver's seat. "Hell," said Collins, "he'd want to pilot the first airplane." Bulova did, in fact, follow up, but Sam told him that the deal was off. The big league extension plan was temporarily tucked away in the abeyance file.

Not long thereafter, the original quadrumvirate of National Airways was reduced to two. After her initial year of hard work in promoting airline sales, Amelia Earhart Putnam began devoting more and more of her time to her personal flying projects, with continuing success. In 1935, she became the first person to fly solo from Hawaii to California, and, later, from Mexico City to New Jersey. Now she set her sights higher. She wanted to make a round-the-world flight, not over the relatively short high-latitude routes, which had been done, but around the equator, a distance of some 27,000 miles, much of it over water. For this, she would need a new airplane, a twin-engine craft instead of the single-engine Vega she had flown on most of her record flights. Amelia had already picked the plane—the Lockheed Electra—and to help finance its purchase she decided to sell her stock in the airline. Of the original foursome, only Sam Solomon and Paul Collins remained active in Boston-Maine Airways.

By the time of the airline's third anniversary, the airline had matured considerably. It had established an excellent safety record under very trying weather conditions. Additional pilots had been hired and more schedules were being flown, including night runs. The line was still not showing a profit, but it displayed promise of edging into the black; traffic volume was growing, steadily if not spectacularly. The time had come to buy some new airplanes, but no more used Stinsons, Collins and Solomon decided. The Stinsons would have to be retained for a while, but to handle the increased passenger traffic they wanted two new modern aircraft. Specifically, they wanted Lockheed Electras.

The Electra was everything the Stinson trimotor was not. The two planes had the same capacity—10 seats— but with two additional planes flying the routes that capacity would be adequate. There the resemblance ended. The Electra, with a top speed of 200 miles per hour, was almost twice as fast as the Stinson. The latter was a fabric covered airplane; the Lockheed plane was all-metal. The Electra had a number of other advantages: complete radio and navigational equipment, essential for efficient operations in New England weather; retractable landing gear; landing lights for night operations. The Electra's two engines had considerably more horsepower than the Stinson's three. It was designed for two pilots instead of one, which would increase the payroll but provide a compensating bonus in safety and flight efficiency. The Electra, in fact, had only one drawback; the two planes needed, plus spare parts, would cost more than $100,000, 20 times what the airline had paid for its original equipment. The airline didn't have the money, but if it was to continue its promising growth, the Electras were a *must*.

So Sam Solomon sought out Lockheed's president, Robert E. Gross, whom he had met before. Gross, a native New Englander who normally operated from his company's main office in Burbank, California, happened to be in Boston visiting his family. At their meeting, Sam spelled out the problem.

Boston-Maine Airways wanted two Electras plus a quantity of spare parts. With the airline's traffic volume growing, the near-future prospects were good; the Electras would permit an approximate doubling of passenger capacity, since their far greater speed would allow more frequent flights than the Stinsons. Thus, the planes would practically pay for themselves. They would have to, Sam concluded, because the airline didn't have the cash to lay out and needed a credit arrangement.

Bob Gross was a sharp businessman and one not inclined to treat lightly the matter of more than $100,000 worth of equipment. But he knew something of Boston-Maine Airways' record and he knew people. He thought a moment, then said simply,

"Will it be all right, Sam?"

"It will be all right," Sam assured him.

Gross stood up and extended his hand.

"That's good enough for me," he said. Thus the Boston-Maine became the first airline to purchase a transport airplane on the installment plan.

Sam arranged that the airline would take delivery of their Electras in Las Vegas, Nevada. There was a good reason for this seemingly odd choice of delivery locale. In California, where the planes were built, there was a state sales tax; Nevada had none. In October, 1936, Sam went to Las Vegas to accept delivery of the first Electra, along with Milton Anderson, who would fly the plane back. They were met at the airport by a Lockheed official and a notary who acknowledged the transfer of title. Then they boarded their gleaming silver Electra and took off for Boston. With its first completely new airplane, Boston-Maine Airways was growing up.

CHAPTER IV

The Battle of Military Road

Is it possible for one man to hold down two full-time jobs simultaneously when the job headquarters are located more than 400 miles apart? One would be inclined to state flatly, "Of course not." Yet Sam Solomon, a man of incredible vigor and tireless enthusiasm for both occupations, did exactly that for almost eight years. Operating from Boston, Sam directed one portion of his energies toward building up the fledgling Boston-Maine Airways. At the same time, he served as manager of Washington-Hoover Airport, one of the nation's busiest air terminals.

Aside from the physical task of moving between the two headquarters, it was a hectic, demanding period in both enterprises, involving pressures that might have sent a lesser man to a rest home. But to Sam Solomon it was just a very interesting phase of his career; to a man who thrives on challenge, two challenges offer double enjoyment.

The second major job—management of the airport—stemmed indirectly from the assistance Sam provided his aviator friends in extricating them from the swimming pool venture. It was in that connection that he made the acquaintance of Frank Russell of National Aviation Corporation, which had assumed ownership of the airport. During and after his swimming pool involvement, Sam became a familiar figure around the air terminal and, about the time he helped launch the New England airline, he became more intimately connected with the airport.

That was in the summer of 1933, when Sam joined with two pilots, J. S. "Jack" Wynne and William E. Payne, to form Air Services, Inc., a charter and sightseeing operation. Sam handled the incorporation of the group, capitalized at $10; Sam contributed one dollar and the others put up $4.50 each. Wynne was named president, Solomon vice president and Payne secretary-treasurer. Air Services, Inc. operated two small passenger-carrying craft offering short-haul private trips and a three dollar sightseeing ride around Washington.

It was a good summer for air sightseeing and the company made a small profit, enough to enable the trio to pay themselves a dividend at the September meeting of the board. The dividend: tickets for each of them to all games of the World Series, in which the Washington Senators were participating that year.

Just prior to the incorporation of Air Services, Inc., the Hoover

Field portion of the airport property had been sold at public auction. It was acquired by National Aviation Corporation, which set up a subsidiary called National Airport Corporation to operate the combined Washington-Hoover Airport as a privately-owned commercial enterprise. Looking for someone to manage the airport, National Aviation's Frank Russell saw an obvious choice: Samuel J. Solomon, a man of noted business acumen who was thoroughly familiar with the airport and who had some—though still slight—aviation experience. Sam was offered the job and he accepted, prompting aviation columnist Bob Ball to write: "Sam Solomon has been around the airport so much and so long that many folks wondered when he was going to become manager. Now he is."

In taking the new job, Sam had no intention of giving up his participation in Boston-Maine Airways. His reason for accepting was a simple one: he needed an income. The partners in the airline venture were paying themselves a salary, but since there were no profits they took it in stock. The stock was appreciating, but it was paper gain; Sam needed a regular salary to keep himself afloat until the airline could pay a more concrete return.

Sam made it clear to Russell and to Edward O. McDonnell, president of National Aviation, that he could not accept the job on a nine-to-five clockpunching basis and that he must be free to pursue his work with Boston-Maine Airways as long as it did not interfere with his management of the airport. Although McDonnell and Russell must have wondered privately just how Sam proposed to manage this double business life, they agreed that he could set his own work schedule.

Thus it was that Sam Solomon, on October 1, 1933, became general manager of Washington-Hoover Airport, vice president of National Airport Corporation and a director of that corporation. Additionally, he was appointed director and vice president of National Air Lines Corporation, another subsidiary of National Aviation formed with the intent of starting an express air service between Washington and New York. The latter operation never got beyond the proposal stage.

Sam sold out his interest in Air Services, Inc.; with two full-time jobs he had no time for an ancillary occupation and in any event he felt it would have been improper to serve as both landlord and tenant at the airport. Jack Wynne also sold out; he was going with the Bureau of Air Commerce as director of airports. Bill Payne, the surviving partner, continued to operate the charter service.

For years thereafter, Sam Solomon was a long-distance commuter, still living in suburban Washington but traveling frequently to Boston to handle his end of the Boston-Maine operation. On occasion he went by air, but air travel in the early thirties left something to be desired from the standpoint of reliability; it was an era that gave rise to the gag line, "If you've time to spare, go by air." So Sam sacrificed professional loyalty for travel efficiency and did most of his commuting by train. The Federal Express, with sleeping-car service, was ideal for his purposes. It departed Washington every evening at eight and arrived in Boston at eight the following morning; the same schedule prevailed for the return trip. Thus, in either city, Sam could work throughout the daytime hours, board the Federal, and be at his desk in the other headquarters at the start of the business day.

The airport that Sam Solomon took over in late 1933 was an amalgamation of what had once been two separate and adjacent airfields located on what is commonly known as the "Virginia side" of the Potomac River between the Highway and Memorial Bridges. The term "Virginia side", however, needs qualification. Part of the airport property was in Virginia's Arlington County and another part came under the jurisdiction of the District of Columbia. No one could say with any authority just where the boundaries lay because they had been drawn in a rather casual manner some 300 years earlier.

It was in 1632 that England's King James I gave George Calvert, the first Lord Baltimore, a land grant that became the province of Maryland. Under the terms of the grant, Lord Baltimore's property extended, on the "Virginia side," to the "high-water mark of the Potomac River." In 1790, the Congress created the district of Columbia, made up of land ceded by both Virginia and Maryland. Technically, therefore, the District's jurisdiction reached to the limits of Lord Baltimore's grant, the high-water mark—as of 1632—on the west bank of the Potomac. But in three centuries the river had changed both course and width, and who was to define the boundaries with any claim of accuracy? The boundary dispute between Virginia and the District of Columbia was to continue throughout the life of Washington Airport, impeding development of the air terminal and causing Sam Solomon a number of headaches.

The airport had begun life in 1926 as Hoover Field, a tiny, 37 1/2-acre, privately-owned plot that served as the base for Washington's original air service. In 1927, development was started on Washington Airport, just across a road from Hoover Field. A former race track provided a 61-acre nucleus which was later expanded to more than 100 acres by land-filling an adjoining marshy area and by razing a former amusement park. The airfields operated independently until 1930, when they were combined in what became known as Washington-Hoover Airport. It was this combined terminal that National Aviation Corporation—and Sam

Solomon—took over in 1933.

When Solomon assumed office, the airport was simply a bumpy, sod field, roughly rectangular, with no paved runways or taxiways and a maximum of 4,200 feet for landings and take-offs. There was a fairly modern terminal containing, in addition to Sam's office, passenger facilities, a snack bar, a weather station and a control tower on the roof. The tower was radio-equipped, but in 1933 that was a superfluity because few of the airplanes operating at the terminal had radio; operational control was signalled by red and green lights.

The airport was served by three airlines: the large and rapidly growing Eastern Air Transport and American Airways, and a smaller company, Pennsylvania Airlines, which later merged into Pennsylvania-Central. Eastern and Pennsylvania had their own hangars; American operated on an open-air basis. National Airport Corporation also had a hangar, where it performed maintenance for the airlines and private operators. Not long after Sam's take-over, Goodyear Zeppelin Corporation started construction of a hangar and dock, located at the Hoover Field end of the property, for its blimps.

In addition to the aviation facilities, the airport corporation leased a corner of its land for use as a commercial dump and rented space to concessionaires, including a custard stand, a hamburger stand and a lounge-restaurant called the Hangar Club. And, of course, there was the swimming pool; it was now operated by National Airport Corporation and thus Sam Solomon became the *ex officio* supervisor of the pool which had been instrumental in starting his career in aviation.

The airport's revenues derived largely from the concessions, from maintenance work and from airport-use fees charged the airlines on the basis of their operational frequencies. Oddly, it was the concessions, particularly the dump and custard stand, which provided the greatest profit. Aviation revenues took second place, despite the fact that the airlines were flying some 70 landings and take-offs daily, ranking Washington Airport among the nation's 10 busiest.

Sam's airport staff, including the maintenance crew, numbered 15 persons. His principal aides were Clyde Holsinger, the highly competent field supervisor, and Helen Williams, a pleasant, matronly woman who assisted Sam with crisp efficiency in the administrative end of the business.

Starting on the day that Sam Solomon first sat at his airport desk and continuing for several years thereafter, his primary headache was the Battle of Military Road. This was a bitter controversy involving several separate governmental jurisdictions, among them the War Department, the Department of Commerce, the Post Office

Department, the Commonwealth of Virginia, Arlington County, the District of Columbia, the National Park Service, the Congress and even the President of the United States. And always, as these jurisdictions clashed with each other, the man in the middle was Samuel J. Solomon.

The battle stemmed from a situation unique among the world's major airports: a federal highway, called Military Road, ran straight through the airport property, bisecting the field where airplanes were constantly landing and taking off. Connecting the Highway Bridge across the Potomac with the Army's Fort Myer a couple of miles to the west, the road had originally been built to afford Army troops easy access to the Capital in case of emergency. The later construction of Memorial Bridge across the Potomac gave the Army a more direct route to the center of Washington, but in the meantime Military Road had become a main artery for civilian use, a heavily-trafficked route used by Northern Virginians commuting to and from jobs in the District of Columbia.

Even at the outset of airport operations, the road presented a hazardous situation, the danger increasing as airliners became bigger and faster. The larger, speedier aircraft needed more room to land and get airborne. More often than not, they had to cross the highway in a high-speed run, wheels on the ground, whether landing or taking off. The rapidly-moving airplane could not stop nor safely turn to avoid collision; it was up to the non-technical judgment of the motorist, who frequently misgauged the speed of an approaching plane, causing a series of near-misses.

Immediately upon his accession to the managerial post, Sam Solomon sought closing of the road. But since it was a federal highway, closure demanded an act of Congress. One bill to that effect was introduced in the House of Representatives, but it got no further than committee hearings. For years thereafter, Congress was to consider and reconsider the problem, invariably deferring it until a later session despite the urgency and despite Sam's frequent pleadings.

Sam Solomon knew it was only a matter of time before a fatal collision occurred. He saw no help forthcoming from any source, so, ever one for direct action, he took matters into his own hands and installed traffic lights on the highway, one on either side of the landing strip. The lights, controlled from the airport tower, halted vehicular traffic when a plane was on or approaching the strip and flashed as soon as the area was clear. Some motorists grumbled at the delay thus occasioned, a foolhardy few flatly ignored the lights, but for the most part the auto-driving public accepted the control lights as a necessary nuisance, one designed for their own protection as well as the safety of airline passengers. For several months it seemed as though Sam had solved the problem.

Late in 1934, just two days after Sam marked his first anniversary as airport manager, the controversy erupted anew. The driver of an Army truck en route to Fort Myer refused to heed a stop signal, drove through the strip zone and narrowly escaped collision with an incoming airplane.

Solomon hotly fired off a protesting letter to the commanding officer of Fort Myer, Colonel Kenyon Joyce, requesting that in the interests of safety the Army instruct its drivers to obey the signals as the majority of civilian motorists were doing.

Colonel Joyce counterattacked. Ignoring the safety aspects involved, he took affront at what he apparently considered an attempt to undermine Army authority. He replied by letter:

"May I ask the date that this light was installed on United States government property, and by what authority such action was taken?" Joyce added that he was referring the matter to the Secretary of War with a recommendation that the Attorney General be asked to prosecute Solomon for closing a federal road.

Nothing came of that recommendation and Sam continued to operate his traffic lights. But the Solomon-Joyce exchange prompted an investigation by the Federal Aviation Commission. Appearing before the Commission, Sam admitted that he had had no authority to install the traffic lights but added that if they were to come down the Army would have to do it.

"I had exhausted every means of either closing Military Road or regulating traffic across the airport," he said. "I had offered the government, without charge, sufficient airport land for a by-pass road around, rather than through, the airport. When nothing happened, there seemed no alternative but to take the matter into my own hands.

"I hope the lights will be permitted to remain," he added. "I think the safety of lives and property more than justifies their existence, even though they are there without authority."

The Commission took no action and the signal lights remained in place, but the controversy took on a new aspect. Aircraft manufacturers were developing a new generation of still larger airliners with cruising speeds around 200 miles per hour, planes which would need all the runway they could get. The Secretary of Commerce, long concerned by the Military Road hazard, informed Sam that he would refuse to permit these new planes to use Washington-Hoover Airport unless complete control of ground traffic could be assured; if only an occasional harebrained motorist ignored the lights, as the Army truck driver had, this constituted insufficient safety precaution in the view of the Department of Commerce.

Thus Sam found himself trapped between the conflicting opinions of two cabinet departments. The War Department wanted the traffic lights eliminated; the Department of Commerce felt that the traffic lights should remain in place but that they should be buttressed by additional safety measures. With no way to appease both agencies, Sam reasoned that his primary obligation was to insure air safety and the Army be hanged. Accordingly, he put guards on the traffic lights and reinforced their authority by providing chain barriers; when the light flashed red, the guards would stretch the fender-height chains across the road, eliminating temptation on the part of the motorist to ignore both guard and traffic light. Commerce found this approach satisfactory; the Army seethed.

While these developments were taking place, Sam Solomon undertook a new program, a quest for a law degree by attending school at nights. It was, he admitted to himself, mostly a sentimental whim, prompted by the long-ago memory of Maggie Solomon's hope that her son would become a lawyer. But the undertaking had its practical side, too. In both his airline and airport operations, particularly during the Battle of Military Road, he had noted many occasions where it would have been advantageous to have had an attorney on the payroll. Why not himself?

Following thought with action, Sam enrolled at George Washington University's evening law school but he soon found that his murderous schedule left no time for a third major endeavor. He was dropped for non-attendance and failure to pass examinations. But, having made the decision to get a law degree, Sam Solomon would not lightly abandon the quest. He enrolled later at National University, another Washington college offering evening courses, and solved the problem of making classes: an acquaintance who worked in the administration office obligingly filled in an occasional attendance card for him.

While operating at the Washington end of his dual existence, Sam saw a great deal of his friend and former partner, Gene Vidal. As director of the Bureau of Air Commerce, Vidal was the government official responsible for maintenance of air safety and the requisite improvement of the nation's airports and airways system. It was a tough, pressure-laden job in an erratic, troublesome period of air transportation growth and Sam noted that Vidal seemed constantly worried. Vidal admitted it. "But," he said one day at lunch, "I'm getting over it. Today I decided not to worry any more because I couldn't remember what I was worried about yesterday."

Vidal shared with Sam the headaches of trying to maintain safety at Washington-Hoover Airport, which was frequently cited as the most dangerous field in the nation. The two teamed in an effort to eliminate one of the airport's major hazards, a network of pole-mounted high-tension power lines strung across the southwest boundary of the field. The power lines reached 30 feet into the air, forcing a pilot coming in for a landing to remain well above them to allow a generous margin of safety. Once past the obstruction, the pilot had to descend quickly at a steeper-than-desirable angle in order to get sufficient room for his landing roll.

The power lines were equally dangerous on take-off, as Sam Solomon knew from first-hand experience. One day, just after testifying before a Congressional committee on the hazard these lines presented, Sam departed for Boston aboard a twin-engine Eastern airliner. Just after take-off, as it approached the power lines, the plane lost an engine. With half its power gone, the airliner climbed sluggishly and it looked for a moment as though the obstruction he had asked Congress to eliminate would claim Sam Solomon as a victim. But the pilot managed to lift his craft over the power lines, just barely, and return to the field for a landing.

Vidal and Solomon met with officials of the Potomac Electric Power Company, briefed them on the technical aspects of operating a high-speed airplane and requested cooperation in removing the hazard. The power company, after a period of considering the costs involved, complied with the request, moving the high-tension lines underground.

Another former partner, Amelia Earhart Putnam, turned up frequently in Washington between record-setting flights. Once Sam arrived at his office to find a message asking that he call the White House. "Forget it," he told secretary Helen Williams, "It's probably one of my drunken friends playing a gag." But when a second message came, Mrs. Williams persuaded him to answer it. It turned out to be Amelia, who was a personal friend of Mrs. Eleanor Roosevelt and who often stayed at the White House during her visits to the Capital.

"Sam," said Amelia, "will you come and get me and take me to lunch? I'm hungry."

"Amelia, you must be kidding," Sam replied. "How can you be hungry at the White House?"

"I am," Amelia insisted. So Sam agreed to take her to lunch. He drove to the White House in the dirty, battered old Ford he used as an airport field car and started up the circular driveway—there were no gate guards in those days and one could drive right to the White House door without challenge. But on approaching the impressive Executive Mansion, Sam had a second thought. Solomon, he said to himself, you can't drive up to the White House in this old wreck. He kept going, parked the car in a garage a few blocks away, returned to the White House in a taxi and met Amelia.

By this time it had started to rain and Sam had unthinkingly dismissed the taxi. Apologetically, he informed Amelia he didn't have his car and he knew no way to get away from the White House, so they would have to walk. "Maybe you'll also be the first White House guest to walk out in the rain," he added.

They walked several blocks to a restaurant, where Amelia ordered a double portion, then walked back to the White House in the rain. Sam felt foolish but Amelia thought the whole affair was uproarious, and she told the story to friends. Inevitably, it reached the newspapers. George Palmer Putnam was immediately on the telephone to Sam; always public-relations conscious, Putnam was disturbed that the President and the First Lady might be annoyed at the publicity. But Eleanor Roosevelt found the story as amusing as Amelia had. She sent a wire to the aviatrix, saying: "Amelia, why didn't you raid the ice-box? I do." Some years later, in her newspaper column "My Day," Mrs. Roosevelt commented on the Amelia Earhart incident and explained how it was possible to be hungry at the White House: "I remember feeding everyone for a time on the same menus that had been worked out for people on relief in the days of the Depression."

On another of Amelia's visits to Washington, Sam escorted her on a visit to the Senate chambers. In an elevator in the Capitol building, they overheard a fellow passenger relating the latest news report: Wiley Post, the colorful one-eyed barnstormer famous for his round-the-world flights, and Will Rogers, the noted humorist and aviation enthusiast, had crashed on a flight to Alaska. Both had been killed.

Amelia was visibly shaken. Both Post and Rogers had been close friends, and the report affected her deeply. And there was something more, Sam thought. "There was something in her reaction," Sam later told friends, "something beyond her obvious grief, that made me feel that perhaps, at that moment, she had a premonition of her own end."

Washington Airport continued to cling tenuously to its no-fatality record, but there were a number of minor accidents. Once, while Sam watched from the field side of the administration building, the slow-moving Goodyear blimp, maneuvering for a docking, got in the way of an American Airlines transport coming in for a landing. The American pilot pulled up his retractable gear and flew around the field for another try. On the second attempt, wheels down again, the pilot was again forced to retract his gear and maneuver around the blimp. By the third pass, the blimp had moved away, but this time the agitated pilot forgot to lower the landing gear. The plane landed on its belly and skidded a long distance across the field. No one was injured but the airplane was severely damaged.

Another accident occurred when an airport employe, who was not a pilot, sought to convince a girlfriend that he was. Late one evening, with the girl in tow, he climbed into the airport's Stinson Reliant parked in the maintenance hangar and somehow managed to start the engine and release the brakes. Unchocked, the plane started to roll. Its wing hooked a wooden post supporting the hangar roof, causing the Reliant to pivot and crash into a brand-new government-owned Beechcraft. Again, no one was injured, but both planes suffered extensive damage.

As it is today, airport noise was a constant headache for Sam Solomon. There were continuing complaints from a number of quarters, the most vehement coming from the sponsors of the Watergate open-air concerts, held just across the Potomac from the airport, directly under the normal take-off pattern. Sam was invited more than once to attend the concerts and hear for himself the racket the airplanes created, and he went, fearing the adverse publicity of his refusal. Oddly, there was never any noise when Sam Solomon was in the audience. On each occasion he took the precaution of leaving instructions with the dispatcher: "Don't route anything over Watergate tonight."

A casual suggestion by Sam Solomon triggered the airline practice of obtaining catered meal service from restaurant chains. American Airlines, among the first to offer on-board food, tried snack-type meals bought from the Hangar Club at the airport. The trial was not very satisfactory and an American Airlines official sought Sam's advice.

"Why not try the Hot Shoppe?" Sam suggested, referring to the nearby restaurant which he frequently patronized. American took up the suggestion and was delighted with the result. In a short time, the Hot Shoppe developed a substantial catering business, for American and other airlines. Today, Marriott Corporation, owner of the Hot Shoppe chain, operates an In-Flite Services Group whose revenues top $100 million annually.

About this time, Sam became embroiled in a new controversy with a new antagonist—the National Park Service. Running along the edge of the airport was a channel, part of which was National Park Service domain and part airport property. With a lot of new government buildings being constructed in Washington, there was an abundance of fill dirt available for nothing. So Sam decided to fill in a part of the channel that belonged to the airport, with no particular purpose in mind except that the reclaimed land might be useful later. The fill was accomplished, hundreds of truckloads of dirt being deposited in the channel to form a potentially valuable extension of the airport land.

Then an irate representative of the National Park Service descended upon Sam Solomon. It seemed that in the filling process Sam had covered up some granite markers which served to mark the boundaries of the park property. This, said the park man, amounted to defacing government property and Sam was therefore subject to prosecution.

Sam thought it was a lot of ado about little. He had seen the granite markers; they were nothing more than small, shaped stones jutting a few inches above the ground. As a budding lawyer, Sam didn't think the Park Service could make much of a case about burying a couple of stones.

"I think I'll make a test case of that," he informed the park man.

"Mr. Solomon," the park man amplified, "you covered more than a hundred of those markers."

"In that case," Sam backed off quickly, "I'd better think it over." He apologized to the park man, who did not seem entirely satisfied. For months thereafter, Sam awaited the government's vengeance, but nothing happened.

On July 8, an incident at the airport brought a new escalation in the Battle of Military Road. A twin-engine Eastern airliner, en route from New York, approached Washington-Hoover Airport in a heavy downpour. With visibility reduced to almost nothing, the pilot overshot the field on his first pass and was forced to go around. On the second try, he managed to touch down, but too far along the landing strip for a normal roll. Forced with a decision as to whether to hit the brakes on the wet, slippery sod or crash into a hangar, the pilot applied brakes. The plane skidded for some distance, then its left wing struck the hangar door, spinning the airplane to a halt. Miraculously, none of the two pilots and five passengers was hurt.

Weather, rather than Military Road, had been the primary cause of the crash, but the road, long damned as a danger spot, got the blame. Sam's chain barriers had proved partially effective, but there were still frequent instances where a motorist breezed through a red light before the guard had time to hook the chain in position. They got away with it because the guards were not police officers, only airport employes with no power to make arrests.

One Washington paper, which quoted no source, said the pilot had overshot because he had tried to "avoid landing on dangerous Military Road." Although any sensible pilot would much prefer to take his chances with road traffic rather than deliberately overshoot, this version gained credence. There was a new uproar in the press, in

Congress and among the public.

Gene Vidal, speaking for the Department of Commerce, stated that Washington-Hoover Airport would have to be closed to airline operations unless the road hazard could be entirely eliminated. The Post Office Department threatened to move airmail operations to Baltimore. Sam Solomon repeated his perennial demand that the road be closed.

Now, however, Virginia's Arlington County took up defense of Military Road. Over the years traffic had built up on the road to the point where its closing would put a heavy load on alternate routes. The county, therefore, publicly opposed the closure and since Arlington had its backers in Congress a new squabble broke out on Capitol Hill.

The argument dragged on for months, well into 1936. One result was the introduction, in both Houses of Congress, of bills calling for the permanent closure of Military Road. Under the provisions of these bills, the Federal government would sell the four-acre strip of roadway running through the airport to National Airport Corporation for $50,000. The money would be given to Arlington County for construction of a substitute road.

Sam Solomon met with the airport corporation's board to consider this compromise, but the proposal was rejected. The stated price of $50,000, or $12,000 per acre, was out of line with the per-acre valuation of airport property.

Suddenly, the War Department injected a new note into the controversy. Unaccountably, the Army now asked the Department of Justice to force the airport corporation to remove its patrol guards from the Federal highway.

Sam Solomon immediately retaliated. Fully aware that his move would bring Department of Commerce action, he announced that he would withdraw his guards five days hence. Commerce reacted quickly, with a statement that removal of the guards would force closure of the airport. Thus, the Army's demand had a backfire effect; the nation's capital was threatened with loss of its airport and it was the Army which had precipitated this intolerable situation.

The controversy was front-page news every day and Sam spent so much of his time answering phone calls that he finally announced to his family that he would not be available to any caller, whoever he was. One night at dinner there was a call and Sam's son Richard, who answered it, suggested that he had better make an exception; there was an Army colonel on the line who sounded important. Sam took the phone.

"I am the aide to General Malin D. Craig," the caller announced.

"The general would like to talk to you."

"Who's he?" Sam asked.

"General Craig," said the colonel, a little testily, "is the chief of staff of the United States Army."

"In that case I'll talk to him," replied Sam, properly impressed.

The general came straight to the point.

"Mr. Solomon," he said, "you have placed the Secretary of War in a very embarrassing position."

"Don't fool yourself, General," Sam retorted. "The Secretary has put me in an embarrassing position." Craig requested a personal meeting and Sam agreed to a next-day conference at the Chief of Staff's office in the State-War-Navy Departments building near the White House.

At the appointed time Sam was ushered into General Craig's office. Sam literally charged into the room, geared for a tough argument, but he pulled up short. The atmosphere was totally impressive: the thick carpeting, the luxurious furnishings, the huge mahogany desk and, behind it, the flag of the United States and the personal flag of the Chief of Staff. Rising to greet Sam was the top military officer of the United States, resplendent in full-dress uniform because he was to attend a funeral later that day. Sam, not one to awe easily, was awed.

"General," he said, "whatever I had on my mind I've changed it." The general smiled and what might have been a hot verbal battle became a pleasant exchange of opinion. In the end, each agreed that he would withdraw his ultimatum and that they would wait for Congress to settle the Military Road dispute.

Soon afterward Congress came up with another compromise measure. It was a resolution, agreeable to all parties, that the road would remain open at all times except during landings and take-offs at the airport; that the airport management would have authority to close the road at such times by means of its traffic lights; that the airport guards would be given authority to arrest violators of the traffic light system; and that the penalty for violations would be a fine of $500, or imprisonment for six months, or both. It was not a completely satisfactory solution as far as Sam Solomon was concerned, but it was better than no solution.

With a higher degree of runway protection thus assured, the airport corporation initiated an improvement program. For the first time Washington-Hoover Airport was to have paved runways, a 4200-foot main runway and a secondary runway of 2800 feet intersecting the main runway in a cross-shaped pattern. Sam Solomon wanted to extend the main runway farther, by means of a landfill in the Boundary Channel, a Potomac inlet adjoining the airport. This, however, was vetoed by the National Capital Park and Planning Commission, on the grounds that the fill would eliminate a recreational area.

By September, 1936, the work of grading the runway areas was completed and paving started. But, despite the improvement program, the days of Washington-Hoover Airport were clearly numbered. Ever since the start of the Battle of Military Road, there had been demands for a completely new and modern airport to serve the nation's Capital. The crash of the Eastern airliner proved the catalyst that solidified public and government opinion in favor of a new air terminal.

It seemed, however, that any proposal with regard to Washington's airport situation was foredoomed to extensive talk, squawk and counter-proposal. Now the question was where should the new airport be located? Right where it is, further expanded, some argued; others proposed sites in nearby—and not so near-by—Virginia and Maryland. The argument waxed hotly for months—and months—and months. Meanwhile, Washington-Hoover Airport went about its business, for all its problems still free of fatality.

Late in 1936, Sam Solomon wound up his legal training at National University. By home study, sandwiched in between airport and airline work, he had managed to pass the required tests. However, he was informed by National University officials, in order to graduate he would have to take two courses which he had overlooked—equity pleading and common law pleading. Sam persuaded the school's administrators to allow him to take "make-up" examinations in these subjects. Once again he attacked the law books at home, passed the tests without ever having had an hour's formal instruction in either subject, and received his law degree.

CHAPTER V
Growing Pains of the Boston-Maine

By the beginning of 1937, Boston-Maine Airways had come a long way from its primitive origins only three and a half years earlier. The two installment-plan Electras were in regular service; within a year they would be joined by five additional planes of the same type, purchased second-hand from Eastern Airlines and National Airlines. The old Stinsons were gradually being retired.

A couple of the original pilots, fed up with New England weather, had departed the scene. They had been replaced by a number of new faces, for the Electras required twice as many pilots as their predecessor transports. Many of the route stations had grown from cow-pasture landing strips to fairly modern airports with paved runways, control towers, radio facilities and airport lighting; night operations were now standard.

In New England, air transportation was gaining more and more acceptance. Passenger volume was approaching the level of 100,000 passenger-miles a month, hardly a staggering figure in comparison with the traffic handled by the larger airlines, but an impressive statistic for a small, short-haul company whose average hop between stations was something in the neighborhood of 50 miles.

There was a concomitant increase in airmail revenues, but despite the gains in both passenger and mail volume, there were still no profits; operating expenses had mounted with growth. Nonetheless, there was light at the end of the tunnel; the growth pattern inspired hope for profitable operations in the not-too-distant future.

On March 1, 1937, the airline underwent a corporate reorganization. To simplify the involved relations between the operating company—National Airways—and the three railroads, all of the assets of National Airways were merged into Boston-Maine Airways and National Airways ceased to exist. In exchange for their assets, the partners in National Airways received half of the common stock of Boston-Maine Airways. Although only Collins and Solomon remained of the four founding partners, the stock payment was split three ways; back in 1933, when Gene Vidal had gone to join the Bureau of Air Commerce, the other members of the quadrumvirate had voted to set aside in Vidal's name a percentage of the stock, until such time as he could return to active participation. Thus, the corporation was now composed of six partners, counting each railroad as one, each partner holding almost-equal shares of more than 16 percent.

In the wake of the reorganization, Sam Solomon began to think again in terms of route expansion and this time he came up with a really grandiose plan: to become the first airline to fly the North Atlantic route to England. Collins liked the idea and together they considered how it could be done. The major problem from the operational standpoint was airplane range and the company's Electras, of course, were not up to the task.

Solomon and Collins, however, were not thinking of an immediate start of service; they were looking farther down the road. The twin-engine Douglas DC-3, the first really efficient commercial airliner was already in service. Airplane designers had moved on to the next step. In early construction status at the plants of the major transport builders were the members of a new generation of airliners. Huge four-engine craft with range capabilities far beyond those of the DC-3, they would be available in a couple of years. Under favorable wind conditions, these four-engine planes would be able to fly non-stop to the British Isles from jumping-off points in Newfoundland or Labrador. At other times, the route could be segmented into easy stage lengths by making refueling stops in Greenland or Iceland.

The big hurdle was to get landing rights in the British Isles. Pan American's Juan Trippe had tried and failed five years earlier, but, Sam argued, perhaps the British attitude had changed in the interim. He proposed that they seek the aid of the man who had interceded for Trippe: S. J. Hungerford, president of Canadian National Railways and a giant of the transportation industry. Hungerford was an indirect participant in Boston-Maine Airways, because Canadian National owned the Central Vermont Railroad, one of the Boston-Maine's five partners.

Solomon and Collins went to Canada to enlist Hungerford's aid. Along with them, the Central Vermont sent its general passenger traffic manager, Ted Pringle. Ostensibly, Pringle's job was to serve as contact man with Canadian National. His real job, Sam thought privately, was to act as public relations monitor of the meeting, to insure that Solomon and Collins did not get out of line with Hungerford, who was regarded with awe by Central Vermont officials.

Hungerford happened to be in Ottawa at the time, testifying at a session of Parliament on the subject of how Canadian National, a government-owned railway, had managed to lose some $60,000,000. Collins, Solomon and Pringle went to Ottawa and checked into the Chateau Laurier, where Hungerford was staying. And there they sat, for several days. Each day Pringle, attempting to contact Hungerford through lower-echelon channels, would report that the president was far too busy with parliamentary matters to see them. Sam Solomon, who was absent from two jobs rather than one, grew impatient. Finally, he said,

"The hell with the proper channels. I'm going to call him directly."

Pringle was horrified; one simply didn't call S. J. Hungerford directly. Sam Solomon, who enjoyed pulling a leg, added:

"Maybe the poor fellow's embarrassed that he can't take us to lunch after losing all that money. I'll tell him we'll buy, we're a solvent company."

"You can't do that," Pringle croaked.

"Watch me," said Sam. He picked up the phone, asked for Hungerford's room and was put through without difficulty. Hungerford greeted Sam pleasantly and accepted his invitation to lunch that same day. Sam made no reference to Canadian National's financial troubles, however, to Pringle's immense relief.

Over lunch, Sam and Paul Collins outlined their plan to fly the North Atlantic, but while Hungerford remained pleasant it was apparent from the outset that he was less than enthusiastic. For one thing, he indicated that he still had a commitment to Pan American's Juan Trippe. When the British were ready to grant landing rights to a North American carrier, Hungerford would see that Pan Am got first consideration. Further, Hungerford was firm in his opposition to the view that the North Atlantic could be flown by land-based aircraft; he had been over this ground before and had been convinced by Trippe that flying boats were the only safe way of crossing the ocean.

Collins argued that flying boats were inefficient carriers in the first place and, more importantly, they posed a major operating problem in the winter, when the waters of the far north iced over. But Hungerford was unyielding; he could not support their proposal nor would he negotiate in their behalf with the British. The turndown amounted to a veto, since Collins and Solomon knew that their American railroad partners would not go along with any proposal rejected by Hungerford.

Reluctantly, Sam Solomon shelved the idea. He did not, however, abandon it; he simply tucked it into a corner of his mind, to be revived at a more propitious time. He knew that some day in the not distant future land-based planes would be flying the North Atlantic route and he was determined that, when the day came, his airline would be in the picture.

The summer of 1937 witnessed a great tragedy, the loss of Amelia Earhart Putnam. Amelia was mourned by all America, but particularly by Sam Solomon, Paul Collins, Gene Vidal, Milton Anderson and the others who had known and worked with her during the airline's first arduous year.

Amelia had gone ahead with her long-time dream of making a round-the-world flight through the equatorial latitudes, which had never been accomplished. Originally, she had planned to make the journey westbound from California, flying in her Lockheed Electra specially modified for the project. The plane had been fitted with two new 1100-horsepower Wasp H engines and in what normally would have been the passenger cabin there had been installed extra fuel tanks, which gave the Electra a maximum range of more than 4,000 miles for the long overwater hops involved.

On March 17, Amelia took off from Oakland bound for Honolulu, accompanied by a three-man crew. Two of them were navigators: Fred Noonan, a top-rated aerial navigator, and Harry Manning, captain of an ocean liner. The third man was the noted stunt flier Paul Mantz, who was not part of the round-the-world crew; he was simply hitchhiking to Honolulu and offered to serve as relief pilot for that first leg of the journey.

Amelia and her team negotiated the transocean hop to Hawaii without incident. On the second leg, however, the Electra suffered an accident on take-off; no one was injured but the plane was too extensively damaged for local repair and it had to be returned to the Lockheed plant at Burbank.

At Burbank, Amelia found it would take three months to rework and retest the airplane, and the delay had other impacts. The original route had been carefully plotted with an eye to prevailing weather; weather conditions three months later would differ considerably, so it became necessary to alter the flight plan. On the second attempt, Amelia would depart the United States eastward from Florida and fly a counter-clockwise route around the world. The change in plan meant that Amelia would have to obtain new clearances from the State Department and the Department of Commerce, so while the Electra was being rebuilt she flew to Washington to contact those agencies. In the Capital, Amelia called Sam Solomon and asked him to visit her at her suite in the Willard Hotel.

When Sam arrived, he found Amelia in bed; she was not feeling well, although it was nothing serious. As they chatted, the telephone rang. It was George Putnam making his daily call to his globetrotting wife.

"How are things going?" Putnam asked.

"Fine," Amelia replied, adding with a chuckle, "I'm in bed and Sam's with me."

"Listen," said Sam, when Amelia had concluded her conversation with her husband, "make sure you straighten that guy out before you take off again."

They talked about her flight. Her new route would take her on multiple stops from Florida through the Caribbean and down the coast of South America to Brazil. Then there would be the transatlantic hop to French West Africa. She would cross Africa to Arabia, India and Burma, then fly through the Dutch East Indies to northern Australia and New Guinea. The last stages of the trip would be island-hopping flights across the Pacific to California. Sam, who had earlier discussed the technical aspects of a round-the-world flight with Paul Collins, had his misgivings; it was an ambitious undertaking for that day.

"Amelia," he asked, "why are you making this flight?"

"Just because I want to," she replied, simply.

"Well," Sam acknowledged, "I don't know any better reason." He took his leave shortly thereafter and that was the last time he saw Amelia Earhart Putnam.

Amelia returned to California, picked up the Electra and in late May started her flight from Oakland, the official departure and return point. This time she was accompanied only by navigator Fred Noonan; Harry Manning had returned to his ship command. The pair flew across the continent to Miami, then, on June 1, left the United States on the first overwater leg of the global journey.

For more than four weeks and 24 stops, Amelia flew her route as planned, experiencing only minor trouble. On June 30, she arrived at Lae on the east coast of New Guinea, having completed roughly three-quarters of the journey.

Three days later, Amelia and Noonan took off from Lae and headed for tiny Howland Island, a United States territory in the Central Pacific Basin 2556 miles from Lae. Near Howland, the cooperating U.S. Coast Guard cutter *Itasca* was standing by to serve as a floating beacon to guide Amelia to the little island.

En route, the Electra's radio developed trouble; it was not completely inoperable, but transmissions were marked by heavy static. The *Itasca* picked up one fairly clear message from Amelia: Noonan's position put them about 200 miles from the island and she requested that the cutter take a bearing on her transmission to provide a more definite fix. However, the transmission was broken and *Itasca* was unable to comply. Amelia tried three more times to establish firm contact, but the messages were so badly distorted by static it was impossible for the ship's radio team to get the bearing. Then there was silence.

For 16 days, ships of the U.S. Navy searched thousands of square miles of the Central Pacific, to no avail. Amelia Earhart Putnam had disappeared without a trace.

Life went on at Boston-Maine Airways. Sam Solomon revived an ambition temporarily deferred two years earlier: extension of the route structure from Boston to New York. By this time, the extension had become a necessity to efficient operation of Boston-Maine Airways. All over its system the airline was boarding passengers whose ultimate destination was New York rather than Boston. At Boston, they had to transfer to American Airlines. But American, experiencing a rapid growth in passenger volume, often could not provide space for the Boston-Maine's passengers. They were forced to finish their journeys by rail, negating the convenience of air travel. To provide complete air service, Boston-Maine Airways had to fly its customers all the way to New York, where they could make connections for any other part of the country.

The extension plan demanded new financing, so once again Collins and Solomon set forth on a quest for backers. They made a great many contacts, but with little success. There were a couple of "almost" deals.

One of the contacts was Richard Hoyt of the investment banking firm of Hayden, Stone & Company, who was also a top executive of Curtiss-Wright Corporation, a leading aircraft and engine manufacturer. Hoyt was interested in the Boston-New York proposal but he wanted to insure that Curtiss-Wright got a piece of the action. He offered backing if the Boston-Maine would fly Curtiss Condor biplane transports, equipped with floats to operate from Boston Harbor to a Hudson River dock near Wall Street in lower Manhattan. Collins and Solomon decided this was not a practical operation, principally because of debris in both landing zones and icing conditions in winter.

They made another presentation, involving several conferences, to H. J. Fuller of Aldred & Company, a banking house. Fuller was obviously impressed by the detailed proposal they presented and it looked for a while as though the Boston-Maine had found its financing. Then Fuller dropped the bomb. Of course they knew, he said, that he was also chairman of the board of Gillette Safety Razor Company—which they hadn't known. It would be Gillette which would be providing the money, Fuller continued, and the company would expect a consideration: for advertising purposes, the airline would be known as the "Blue Blade Line."

Paul Collins took a minute to digest that pronouncement, then stood up abruptly.

"Sam," he said, "let's get the hell out of here. We'd be tagged all over the industry with 'Every ride a close shave.'"

In their search for financing, Solomon and Collins, along with

Gene Vidal, were invited to the home of a New York banker for a business dinner. Throughout the dinner, Collins held forth animatedly on the economic potential of the Boston-New York route. They reached the dessert course and the butler served each a dish of strawberries, then handed Paul the sugar. Collins, delivering his sales pitch with eyes fixed on the banker, absently sprinkled sugar on what he thought was the strawberry dish but was in fact his finger bowl. The butler pretended not to notice and offered Collins the cream pitcher. Still talking and totally engrossed in his subject, Paul proceeded to pour the cream into the finger bowl until it ran over. The banker studiously looked elsewhere; the butler wore a pained expression. Suddenly aware of his gaucherie, Collins was abashed. This was an indication of an intense concentration and effort.

Afterwards, he turned on Solomon and Vidal.

"Why didn't you tell me what I was doing?" he asked them.

Gene shrugged and said innocently,

"We thought you liked them that way."

Nothing came of that meeting, nor of several others. The Boston-New York plan hung fire.

In the spring of 1938, New England suffered heavy floods. Rivers overflowed, knocking out rail and road bridges; many communities were isolated as surface transportation was choked off. To supply the cutoff areas, Boston-Maine Airways went on emergency status, flying around the clock, hauling food, medicines and other necessities in the Electra fleet. American Airlines also joined in the relief effort. It was a grand performance, and when the floodwaters abated New England was duly appreciative, perhaps realizing for the first time the community-aid value of its airlines. Apparently, New Englanders were also impressed by the reliability of air operations as demonstrated in the flood service; traffic volume thereafter mounted at a greater rate than previously.

In the summer of 1938, the Congress passed the Civil Aeronautics Act, establishing the first really comprehensive system of regulating aviation in the United States. The Act created the Civil Aeronautics Authority, a governmental agency with three main subdivisions. One group took over the functions formerly handled by the Department of Commerce with regard to promulgating air safety rules and operating the navigation facilities of the national airways system. A second group, the Air Safety Board, was charged with investigating aircraft accidents with an eye toward learning the causes and making recommendations for new safety regulations. The third group was responsible for economic regulation of the airlines. The latter two groups were later merged into an independent agency known as the Civil Aeronautics Board.

The Act's major impact on the airlines came in the area of route extensions. No longer was it possible to start a new route simply by obtaining the permission of the communities involved; henceforth route awards were to be controlled by the Civil Aeronautics Authority, and later the Civil Aeronautics Board, on the basis of economic viability. A route might profitably support one airline, but not two or more; competition had to be restricted because the airlines were getting government subsidy and their economic health was therefore a matter of government concern. So the awarding of new routes became a matter of formal application, extensive government study of potential traffic and other economic considerations, hearings before an examiner and a lengthy period of post-hearing deliberation. Some route proceedings dragged on for several years.

That, in fact, is what happened to Boston-Maine Airways' request for the long-considered Boston-New York route. The airline filed its application shortly after the creation of the Civil Aeronautics Authority, but it was to be more than five years before the regulatory body—by that time the Civil Aeronautics Board—delivered its decision.

The Civil Aeronautics Act had another influence on Boston-Maine Airways. It seems incredible in retrospect, but prior to 1938 there was no formal requirement that an airline pilot demonstrate his ability to fly by instruments. Following passage of the Act, the Civil Aeronautics Authority instituted a regulation that all transport pilots must be instrument-rated. The agency set up an instrument-flight training school in Detroit and Milton Anderson was nominated to be Boston-Maine Airways' first trainee.

Anderson went through two courses at the school, once as trainee and once as instructor. On his return to the airline, he persuaded Collins and Solomon that the Boston-Maine should set up its own instrument school. The airline acquired space in the Boston terminal, bought an instrument ground trainer and, with Anderson as instructor, started training pilots. This, the first airline-operated training school, became the nucleus of a much broader instructional program conducted by the airline in later years.

In August, 1939, Boston-Maine Airways sought another route, this time to Moncton, New Brunswick, some 200 miles northeast of Bangor. It was a logical extension of the airline's route structure, one which offered connecting service to other points in Canada via Trans-Canada Air Lines and Canadian Airways. To Collins and Solomon, it was something more than that; they had never completely dropped the idea of flying the North Atlantic to Europe. Moncton represented a foot in the door, an intermediate station between Bangor and Newfoundland, the potential jumping-off point for the

North Atlantic route.

Only days after the filing of the application, the Moncton extension took on new meaning. On September 1, Germany invaded Poland; Britain and France immediately declared war on Germany. This was the formal start of the second World War, which had been brewing for years in Europe.

The United States initially adopted a policy of neutrality, stating, however, that it would take steps to defend the Western Hamisphere against totalitarian aggression. A man of more penetrating vision than most of his countrymen, Sam Solomon felt it would be impossible for the U.S. to maintain complete neutrality; defense of the Western Hemisphere would entail, at the very least, provision of supplies and war materiel to America's friends in Europe. When that came to pass, the bulk of the logistics effort would naturally be transported by ship, but there would be a need for air movement of certain priority supplies. The shortest and quickest airway to Europe was the Great Circle route from Canada over the North Atlantic. Thus, Sam's earlier plan for a trail-blazing commercial route to Europe had acquired new coloration; in his opinion it would find important utility in defense.

In the normal course of events, Solomon figured, the Civil Aeronautics Authority would take a couple of years or more to deliberate the Moncton extension request. Seeking to accelerate the schedule, he sought the help of the Army Air Corps. He reasoned that Air Corps support, in the form of a statement that the Moncton extension represented the first step in a development of military significance, would bring more rapid action on the part of the regulatory board. Accordingly, he took his case to the Army and was directed to the office of an Assistant Chief of the Air Corps, a brigadier general.

To the general, Sam outlined his views on the North Atlantic route, feeling that his presentation was somewhat superfluous; surely the Air Corps knew better than he the potential of the Great Circle route. To Sam's utter amazement, the Assistant Chief airily dismissed the matter of air supply over the North Atlantic. If it came to an all-out emergency, the general told Sam, there would be no flying activity whatever in the Northeast. The entire East Coast, for some 200 miles inland, would be a restricted area; all radio stations would be shut down lest German bombers use them as navigational aids, homing on their signals. There were, of course, no German bombers capable of flying the ocean, not then or at any time during the war. But the Assistant Chief had spoken and that was the end of it. Sam left the meeting bewildered and disgusted at Air Corps myopia.

Within a few months, events took the course that Solomon had predicted. The United States relaxed its neutrality doctrine and began supplying the Allies in Europe. The urgency of the industrial mobilization under way brought into clearer focus the potential of the North Atlantic route as an aerial supply bridge and the possibility that commercial carriers might play a part in the logistics effort. Without further prodding from Solomon, someone in the Air Corps dusted off Sam's earlier proposal and recommended to the Civil Aeronautics Authority that Boston-Maine Airways be granted the Moncton extension in the national interest. The route was assigned in relatively short order.

Meanwhile, the expansion of the U.S. military services was gaining momentum; reserve personnel were being called to active duty and a full-scale recruitment program was under way. It now appeared to Sam Solomon that the United States was headed for a more active role in the conflict than its current status as the "arsenal of democracy." Sam's patriotic instincts demanded that he offer his services to the Army.

As was his custom, he went straight to the top. On June 10, 1940, he wrote General George C. Marshall, Army Chief of Staff "on the chance that my experience as an airport manager and airline officer may be of some value under present conditions."

He received a surprisingly prompt reply. "Your patriotic tender of service is appreciated," General Marshall wrote, but he pointed out that although rearmament was in progress there was still no formal national emergency. Peacetime regulations were in effect and under those regulations Sam's appointment was "precluded." Technically, Sam was still a second lieutenant in the Field Artillery Reserve, although his commission was inactive. At 40, he was beyond the maximum age limit for that rank, in either the Field Artillery or the Air Corps. Sam was disappointed, but, as things turned out, he was later to play a far more important part in the war effort than he could have played as an individual officer.

Meanwhile, Boston-Maine Airways continued to grow. By mid-1940, traffic volume had risen to more than 250,000 passenger miles a month and it was mounting rapidly. During the busy summer months, the airline was getting more requests for reservations than could be accommodated by the 10-passenger Electras. The number of daily flights was increased, but even this measure could not fully satisfy the demand.

Clearly, there was a need for a new and larger type of airplane. No deliberation was needed as to which type; the Douglas DC-3, now the standard airliner employed by all the major transport companies, was the obvious answer.

The DC-3 had a normal capacity of 21 passengers plus their baggage, but for Northeast's purposes capacity could be increased. In those adolescent days of airline service, when airplane payloads were infinitesimal in comparison with what they would someday become, take-off weight was always a critical matter. To insure against overloading, it was the practice of the airline to weigh not only the baggage, but the passenger as well. Experience showed that Boston-Maine Airways had a considerably lower average passenger/baggage weight than other airlines, not because its passengers were smaller but because of the lesser baggage requirement over the airline's short-haul route structure.

Therefore, for Boston-Maine operations, capacity of the DC-3 could be increased to 24 seats without exceeding the DC-3's payload of 5,000 pounds. By keeping the Electras in supplementary service, Collins and Solomon felt that they could handle the increasing traffic load, for a time at least, with three DC-3's.

The problem, once again, was money. The price tag on the DC-3 was more than $120,000 per airplane; three planes, plus the necessary stock of spare parts, would require an outlay in the neighborhood of $400,000. Although the original Electra purchases of 1936 had seemed a staggering expenditure, re-equipping with DC-3's would cost roughly four times as much.

In Solomon's view, there was only one way to obtain the requisite capital: by offering the airline's stock to the public. Paul Collins disagreed at first; he feared that a public stock sale would erode the control of the airline which he and Solomon had enjoyed since the start of operations. In the end, he deferred to Solomon, as he always did in business matters. The railroads, too, accepted the idea and plans were formulated for a recapitalization program.

As a preliminary step, the name of the airline was changed on the theory that a title more properly reflective of the company's operations would enhance the sale of stock. The airline was flying not simply from Boston to Maine, but throughout New England and into Canada, with a route extension to New York a near-future probability. Accordingly, on November 16, 1940, the Boston-Maine officially became Northeast Airlines.

On January 8, 1941, more than 100,000 new shares of common stock were offered to the public at $4.60 a share. The offering, handled by the Lee Higginson Corporation of Boston, was quickly sold out, providing enough funding for the three DC-3's plus a margin for operating capital. In the stock reshuffle, the three railroads together wound up with 40 percent of the common stock, while Collins, Solomon and Vidal collectively held one-quarter. The remainder went to the public.

In the spring of 1941, Paul Collins decided to resign as president of Northeast; he had been in poor health for some time and he felt he could no longer effectively perform the duties of the presidency at a time when the airline was experiencing surging growth. At a meeting on May 7, Collins was named chairman of the board. Sam Solomon was elected president. Milton Anderson, who was regarded by Solomon as the principal reason for the high caliber of Northeast's flight operations, became vice president.

Less than two months later, Northeast introduced service with the DC-3's. With them came another innovation: the airline's first stewardesses, seven of them, who earlier had completed a four-week training course.

One of the stewardesses created a contretemps. She persuaded the captain of one flight to let her handle the controls of the DC-3, which was absolutely contrary to regulations. The pilot trimmed the airplane for easy level flight, then both he and the copilot retired to the passenger cabin, leaving the stewardess alone in the cockpit. Word of the incident filtered back to Sam Solomon, who was outraged at so flagrant a breach of discipline. He fired all three participants. A few months later, at a hearing on the matter which took place just after the Japanese had attacked Pearl Harbor, Sam reinstated all three offenders. "You are more important to your country in the cockpit," Sam told the pilot.

While these events were transpiring, Northeast's pilot training school was growing into a substantial operation. The big impetus came with the national mobilization, when the government realized that there was a scarcity of trained pilots and that a quick remedy was in order if the nation was to prepare properly for an emergency. Aside from the separate programs of the Army and the Navy, a Civilian Pilot Training Program was instituted under the auspices of the Civil Aeronautics Authority.

Under this program, thousands of young civilians were enrolled for flight training in basic and advanced courses. Funding was provided by the Federal government and the training was conducted by privately-operated flight schools under contract to the CAA. Northeast Airlines, which as Boston-Maine Airways had led the way in setting up an airline training school, was among the first to receive a contract for advanced training of civilian pilots.

To run the school, Northeast hired Ben Cole, a veteran flyer whose experience dated back prior to World War I. Cole expanded the original concept—instrument training only—to include classroom and flight training in a number of additional subjects required by the CAA: meteorology, communications, propulsion systems, radio navigation and celestial navigation.

Cole did an excellent job of reorganizing and expanding the school, but when it came time, in 1941, to renew his contract, Sam Solomon balked. Cole's contract, signed when Paul Collins was president, gave him 10 percent of the training school's gross income. Sam notified Cole that he could not in conscience continue this arrangement; the school's income was coming entirely from government contracts and Sam felt it improper that anyone should have a flat percentage deal where taxpayers' money was involved, particularly at a time when war was imminent.

Cole refused to sign any other type of contract. It was a matter of principle, he said; he had come to the airline with a firm understanding and he insisted on continuance of the percentage agreement.

"Look," Sam told him, "it's a matter of principle with me, too. A percentage deal on a government contract is not good policy, especially at this time. I'm willing to pay you, instead, twice as much as I am getting as president of the airline." Cole remained obdurate. So did Solomon. In the battle between two strong-willed personalities, the outcome amounted to a draw. Cole's contract expired and he left the airline. Ben Follett, who had been assistant to Cole, took over direction of the school, under the supervision of Milton Anderson.

In November, 1941, Sam Solomon filed an application with the government regulatory body—by now the Civil Aeronautics Board—for an extension of Northeast's route from Moncton to St. John's, Newfoundland. This would extend the airline's system all the way to the departure point for the overwater segment of the North Atlantic route. The British were already using the route, flying American-built medium-range bombers under their own power, delivering them to their ultimate destinations in a matter of days rather than the three months surface transportation would require. The next logical step would be cargo movement over the route and, with military transports in short supply, it appeared probable that commercial carriers would be asked to participate. Although circumstances had changed considerably since 1937, when he had initially pursued the dream, Sam Solomon was still determined that his airline would be the first to fly the North Atlantic route.

CHAPTER VI

The Decline of Washington-Hoover Airport

While Sam Solomon the airline executive was pushing expansion of Northeast Airlines, Sam Solomon the airport manager was presiding over the slow demise of Washington-Hoover Airport.

By early 1937, the various agencies involved had finally agreed on a site for a new, modern airport to serve the nation's Capital. It was to be built at Gravelly Point, only a little more than a mile down the Potomac from Washington-Hoover Airport. The main advantage of this site was elbow room; there was land available for lengthier runways and for future expansion, which could not be accommodated at Washington-Hoover Airport.

As usual, however, airport development in the Capital moved at snailpace. Although engineering surveys were being conducted, there was no formal go-ahead for construction.

Washington-Hoover Airport was to remain in business until the new airport was actually built and ready for operations, and that appeared to be a matter of several years.

In the spring of 1937, Sam Solomon became a fully-accredited lawyer. It came as something of a surprise. Months earlier, Sam had taken examinations for admission to the District of Columbia bar, but the results were a long time coming and in the press of other business the matter had been relegated to a remote corner of his mind, almost completely forgotten.

Sam arrived at the airport one day in April and the switchboard operator had a message for him:

"Someone called, I didn't get his name, he said to tell you that you passed."

"Passed what?" Sam asked. The operator didn't know. Neither did Sam until he picked up his newspaper the following morning and found his name among those admitted to the bar.

Publicly, Sam was inclined to belittle the accomplishment.

"In all the history of the District of Columbia," he told friends, "I am probably the least-qualified person ever to pass the bar."

Privately, though, he was pleased. His admittance amounted to a memorial to Maggie Solomon, who had cherished the dream that her son would become a lawyer. And, actually, Sam was not as ill-qualified as he made out. Although his personal appearances at National University had been so infrequent that he barely knew the names of his instructors, Sam had not only passed the bar examinations but had also passed the academic tests required for credits, testimony to the efficacy of his home-study effort. Since he had the type of retentive mind that holds forever a fact once grasped, Sam had acquired some knowledge of the law despite his casual approach to formal training. Although he was never to practice law actively, his sporadic legal education was to prove helpful in his aviation work, in appearances before the Civil Aeronautics Board, state aviation commissions and other regulatory bodies.

A new crisis arose at the airport in July of 1937. Paving of the runways had been completed months earlier and the main runway was adequate for airline operations, but, with the introduction to service of the Douglas DC-3, big and fast for its day, the 2800-foot secondary runway—used when wind conditions dictated—presented a problem; it was simply too short for a safe take-off with a full load. Airline pilots rebelled; they set a 60-day deadline for federal action on a new airport, failing which they would no longer fly into Washington-Hoover Airport.

Of course, no government action was forthcoming; the way Congress approached any matter connected with the airport, 60 days was barely enough time to digest the problem.

In the interim, however, the War Department came up with a partial solution; it offered use of the Army's Bolling Field, a few miles down the Potomac on the other side of the river, as an alternate air terminal. Airliners would continue to use Washington-Hoover Airport's main runway when wind conditions permitted, but when the winds were such as to dictate use of the short runway, the planes would operate from Bolling instead.

The pilots and the airlines accepted this proposal, which exchanged the safety problem for a new one. Passengers waiting to board an incoming airliner would suddenly find that their flight had landed at Bolling. There would be a mad scramble for the available taxicabs and a wild, five-mile dash through southeast Washington to reach the other terminal in time. The use of Bolling Field was not an everyday occurrence, but it happened often enough to make passengers wonder if air travel was really worth the effort; airline traffic suffered, particularly on the Washington-New York run, where the train offered greater convenience at not much sacrifice of time. Incredibly, this situation persisted throughout the remaining years of Washington-Hoover Airport.

The Battle of Military Road was at last winding down. Congress had struck the proper note a year earlier when it proposed sale of the airport section of the highway to National Airport Corporation. The only hurdle remaining was the matter of price; Solomon and his directors could not accept the $50,000 figure originally stated.

Discussions were renewed early in 1938 and Congress came up with a new bill, halving the price to $25,000, the money to be paid to Arlington County for construction of an alternate road. This was agreeable to National Airport Corporation and the bill was passed in April, 1938. Sam Solomon promptly delivered a check to Arlington County—which, incidentally, never got around to building the new highway—and on May 17 barricades were erected, permanently closing Military Road.

Although the opening of a new highway is frequently attended by a ribbon-cutting ceremony, rarely is there any fanfare involved in the closing of a road. In this instance, however, the long notoriety of Military Road seemed to call for some special attention to its demise. A brief ceremony was held at the barricade, Sam Solomon posing for newspaper photographs with the Fort Myer commandant, Colonel Jonathan M. Wainwright, who, as a general, later directed the heroic defense of Bataan Peninsula in the early days of World War II.

Thus, a long-standing headache was eliminated, but Washington-Hoover Airport was fated never to be problem-free for any length of time and Sam soon found himself embroiled in a new argument. This time the antagonist was Eastern Airlines, specifically Eastern's colorful president Captain Eddie Rickenbacker, America's top ace in World War I and a leading figure in postwar civil aviation.

It had come time for Eastern to renew its contract with Washington-Hoover Airport and a dispute arose as to how much Eastern would pay the airport corporation. Normally such negotiations were handled by National Aviation Corporation's headquarters staff in New York, but there was a public relations problem: as an investment company, National Aviation could not afford to antagonize General Motors, which controlled the airline. So Sam Solomon was nominated to lock horns with Eastern and Rickenbacker.

It was an interesting match-up, Solomon vs. Rickenbacker, two tough-minded personalities, each convinced his position was right, neither disposed to compromise. As might be expected, there was no headway in the negotiations. The argument stretched over months, Rickenbacker refusing to pay any fee whatever until the matter was settled.

The situation reached a point where Sam Solomon, at the direction of the airport corporation's board, had to take some kind of action. The airport needed the revenue that Eastern would normally have been paying; although it was operating in the black, it could not afford to carry a major tenant for months without a fee. So Sam wired Rickenbacker to the effect that he would file suit if agreement was not reached by a stated deadline. The return wire from Rickenbacker was prompt and succinct:

"Sue and be damned."

Sam sued. As the time for the trial approached, Eastern, through a Virginia attorney, requested an extension of two weeks to answer the suit. Absolutely not, said Solomon. "This thing has dragged on for months," Sam added, "and I can't see any reason for an extension now."

"There is a reason," the attorney replied. "If I don't get an extension, I don't get a fee."

"Well, that's altogether different," said Sam Solomon, agreeing to the extension. It proved a sound decision; before the time expired, Rickenbacker bent a little, a compromise was reached and the suit was dropped.

Sam Solomon was also involved in a court action with another of aviation's great names: J. H. "Jimmy" Doolittle, an Army Reserve flyer who owned just about every speed record in the book and who, in World War II, was to become doubly famous as leader of the first air raid on Tokyo and later as commanding general of the Eighth Air Force in Europe. Flying promotional flights for Shell Oil Company, Doolittle flew into Washington-Hoover Airport and had an accident on his landing roll.

At the time, Sam Solomon was in Montpelier-Barre airport in Vermont en route to Burlington where he was to make a talk to his airline employees. He was called to the telephone. It was Helen Williams, his secretary in Washington Airport.

"Major Doolittle just cracked up," she reported, adding that she was being besieged by newspaper photographers who wanted to take pictures of the airplane.

"Was he hurt?" Sam asked. He knew and thought very highly of amiable Jimmy Doolittle.

"No. He dashed off in a taxi saying he was going to a funeral."

"As long as it wasn't his own, we don't have a problem," Sam said. Helen asked should she allow the photographers to take pictures. "Sure," Sam replied, "we didn't crack it up."

Later, back in Washington, Sam found that he did have a problem after all. Shell Oil had filed suit against the airport, asking for a substantial sum on the grounds that the accident had been caused by a hole in the runway.

On the day of the trial, Sam received a call from Jimmy Doolittle.

"Sam," Doolittle said, "I'm taking a taxi to the courthouse. Shall I come by and pick you up? After all, there's no skin off us. It's just my insurance company suing yours."

On the way to Arlington Court House, where the case was to be heard, Sam asked Doolittle whose funeral he had attended. Doolittle looked puzzled until reminded of his remark on hastily departing the airport after his accident.

"Oh," He grinned his famous grin. "There was no funeral. I was heading for the Carlton to get a drink. Wouldn't you?"

As a witness for his company, Doolittle told the story of the crash tersely and articulately. It was obvious that he had made a fine impression and Henry Quinn, attorney for the airport corporation, was ready to admit defeat. He leaned toward Sam.

"I think we've lost this case. I can't think of any questions to ask him."

"Ask him whose fault it was, his or the airport's," Sam suggested.

Quinn didn't think much of the idea.

"He'll say it was the airport's fault, of course." Sam thought otherwise. Doolittle was known as a man of exceptional honesty and Sam was betting on Doolittle's integrity, whatever the answer.

"You think you've already lost the case," he said to Quinn, "so what do you have to lose?" Quinn put the question to Doolittle.

"Well," Doolittle replied, scratching his head and looking sheepish, "it was partly the airport's fault and partly mine." The judge immediately threw the case out of court.

It was about that time that Sam Solomon had an interesting flight experience. He was picked up at Washington-Hoover by Paul Myers, a Bureau of Air Commerce official who was piloting a Bellanca Airbus monoplane. Both Sam and Myers were en route to Montpelier, Vermont, to attend a meeting on expansion of the Montpelier-Barre airport. Myers landed at Miller Field, Staten Island, for refueling and while the plane was being gassed Sam dubiously studied the weather. With rain, low clouds and limited visibility it didn't look too good to him.

"How about this weather?" he asked Myers.

"Oh, it's fine, fine," said the Bureau man. With Myers, it seemed, the weather was always fine. Sam, who laid no claim to being a weather expert, did not argue the point.

They took off in the Bellanca and flew up the Hudson River. The weather, it seemed to Sam, was getting worse. Myers was flying very low to stay under the weather and suddenly there loomed in front of the plane the towering superstructure of the George Washington Bridge. There wasn't time to climb over it; Myers simply flew under the bridge. Paul Collins was furious when he learned of the incident later, but Solomon, the non-pilot, had not been at all disturbed.

Myers and Sam eventually reached Montpelier, but late because of weather troubles. They were met at the airport and driven to a house in town, which proved to be a restaurant-guest home operated by the National Life Insurance Company, host for the airport conference. He had missed the scheduled luncheon, Sam found; a man was already clearing dishes from the tables. Sam was introduced to the man, Fred Howland, whom he presumed to be the restaurant proprietor.

Later, after the conference, Sam was asked if he had met Fred Howland; Howland might be helpful in opposing construction of the Gravelly Point airport in Washington. Sam was puzzled.

"How can a Montpelier restaurant man help me in Washington?" he wanted to know.

The "restaurant man," it turned out, had only been clearing dishes to lend a helping hand to his employes. Fred Howland was in fact the president of National Life Insurance Company, one of the most influential men in New England and one who was very close to the Vermont Congressional delegation.

But it was too late for anyone to help prolong the life of Washington-Hoover Airport; an incident in the summer of 1938 tolled its death knell. President Roosevelt had a nightmare. He dreamed that he looked out from his White House bedroom window and saw an airliner crash at Washington-Hoover Airport. The next day he took action; he sent directives to all the agencies involved ordering an end to the procrastination that had for years characterized airport development in Washington. The President wanted a new, ultramodern airport at Gravelly Point that would make the Capital "the hub of transportation by air." To get the ball rolling, he allocated money from a federal emergency fund. Within three months, much of the planning work had been accomplished and construction started.

The decision had no immediate effect on Washington-Hoover Airport. Construction time for the Gravelly Point project was estimated at two years, an estimate which later proved to be optimistic. In the interim, Washington-Hoover Airport was to continue as the air terminal for the nation's capital.

Mid-1939 witnessed a milestone of sorts for Washington-Hoover; the first landing of a four-engine airliner. The plane was a Douglas DC-4, slated for use by United Air Lines, one of the newer tenants of the airport. This was the initial version of the DC-4, the plane that was to become the workhorse of the Army Air Force's heavy transport fleet during World War II and the standard long-range airliner of the immediate postwar years. The original model featured an innovative design in the tail section, which was composed of three separate vertical fins and rudders; this arrangement did not prove entirely satisfactory and in later models of the DC-4 Douglas went back to the conventional single fin and rudder.

The DC-4 was a curio for that day and its arrival attracted a crowd. The event was only slightly marred by the fact that pilot Benny Howard had to land on the short runway because of wind conditions and he burned out the brakes trying to bring the big plane to a halt before he ran out of runway.

In July, 1939, Sam Solomon marked his 40th birthday with a quiet observance at home. Despite the extraordinary demands of his double business existence, Sam still managed an almost normal home life; no matter where the two jobs took him, he made it a point to spend at least the week-end at the Silver Spring family home. The house itself had been substantially enlarged, a huge attic remodeled to incorporate three additional bedrooms for the Solomon's three sons, the eldest of whom was now in high school. The spacious grounds now included a tennis court and a generous-size swimming pool, where Sam on occasion pursued the athletic urge he had never lost. The Solomon home was the scene of frequent gatherings of the aviation clan, at oyster roasts with a hundred or more guests or at less populous week-end "open house" sessions. The attendance list at the Solomons' parties read like a Who's Who of aviation, but there was one rule: only friends were invited, never business contacts, unless— as was most often the case—they were also friends.

At Christmastime in 1939, the employees of Washington-Hoover Airport—by now numbering about 30—took up a collection and bought their boss a present, a huge ornamental mirror embossed by a protuberant model of a DC-3 airliner. The mirror symbolized the solid working relationship that existed between employees and employer during Sam's tenure as airport manager. Mr. Sam was a demanding boss, but known to all as a square-dealer with a genuine solicitude for his employees' welfare.

It was that solicitude that prompted him to make a proposition to the Civil Aeronautics Administration early the following year. The end of Washington-Hoover Airport was now clearly in sight and Sam was concerned about the job prospects of his employees. He sought out the head of CAA's airport section—Major (later four-star general) Lucius D. Clay, an Army officer on detached service with the civilian agency—and offered to take himself out of consideration for the managership of the new airport if the CAA would guarantee to take care of his people when Gravelly Point opened for business.

Clay said he was not in a position to accept such a proposal so Sam, determined, went to Civil Aeronautics Administrator Clinton

Hester. There he found a more sympathetic ear. Hester assured Sam—and later lived up to it—that all employees of Washington-Hoover Airport would be offered jobs at the new terminal. Sam kept his part of the bargain—he did not seek the managerial post. If he had, he would have been confronted with a tough decision; management of the new airport was a Federal position and under the law a Federal executive could not also be an officer of an airline. So, had he sought the job and been accepted, Sam would have been forced to make a choice between management of the world's most modern airport or the continuing challenge of building a major airline.

With the employees guaranteed job security, there remained only one other major matter: disposal of the airport itself. That proved to be no problem; the National Capital Park and Planning Commission, always ready to annex an acre anywhere, wanted the land and suggested a price of $1 million. Sam Solomon was not enthusiastic about the offer; he felt that the property, close to downtown Washington in a period of accelerating growth for the Capital, should be worth considerably more than a million. In the end, however, he had to bow to the majority view of the National Airport Corporation board. In 1940, the government was granted an option to buy the land for $1 million and the option was later exercised.

Although it was moribund, Washington-Hoover Airport experienced its greatest period of growth in the years following the go-ahead for construction of the new Gravelly Point terminal. By mid-1941, it had become the third busiest airport in the world, trailing only New York and Chicago. In addition to private, charter and sightseeing flights, there were some 180 arrivals and departures of airliners every day and traffic flow was averaging about 2,500 passengers a day.

Meanwhile, work progressed at the $15 million Gravelly Point facility, which had acquired a new name: Washington National Airport. By early fall of 1940, the main runway had been completed and it was time to lay the cornerstone for the terminal building.

In a September 29 ceremony attended by some 75,000 people, President Roosevelt personally slapped a ceremonial trowel against the cornerstone. Then, sitting in his open limousine near the taxi ramp, the President triggered a radio signal directing the landing of the first airplane to touch down on Washington National Airport. The plane, a silver Electra operated by the Civil Aeronautics Administration, had made a one-mile flight from Washington-Hoover Airport; on board, along with several top-ranking government aviation officials, was Sam Solomon. Alma Solomon was accorded a similar honor, Departing a few minutes later from Washington-

Hoover, she was one of the passengers of an American Airlines DC-3 which became the first *commercial* aircraft to set down at the new terminal. The opening ceremonies were concluded by a fly-over of more than 500 military and commercial planes, the largest air armada ever assembled in the United States.

Although the airport had been formally commissioned, it was not ready for regular service. But construction moved swiftly thereafter. By year-end, all of the runways, taxi strips and aprons had been paved and most of the technical facilities were ready. The terminal building was completed early in 1941 and finally a date was set for the transfer of all operations to Washington National—June 16, 1941.

The end had come for Washington-Hoover Airport and the Washington Post wrote a fitting obituary, one which reflected the extraordinary effort of Sam Solomon and his small staff:

"Although sharply criticized by world aviation leaders as utterly inadequate to serve the needs of the Capital, Washington-Hoover Airport has enjoyed a safety record almost without parallel among the world's important air terminals. There never has been a fatal airline accident at the field and very few resulting in material damage. For many years it has been regarded as one of the most efficiently managed airports in the world and is one of the very few, public or private, which has been consistently 'out of the red'."

Shortly before midnight on June 15, Sam Solomon climbed to the control tower to dispatch personally Eastern Air Lines' Trip 5, Miami-bound and commanded by Captain J. Olin King. There was no fanfare, no farewell speech, just the briefest of commentaries. "This is the last scheduled flight from Washington-Hoover Airport," Sam radioed King. "Good luck to you."

At intervals over the next few months, Sam continued as the sole employe of Washington-Hoover Airport, handling the paper work involved in the termination and disposing of usable equipment. On September 13, 1941, came the final transaction: Sam was presented a Treasury check in the amount of $1 million in payment for the land. A million was still an enormous sum in those days and the local newspapers ran photos of the check, mentioning Sam as recipient. Sam became more popular than he had ever been, for although the check was clearly marked payable to National Airport Corporation, nearly everyone got the impression that it was Solomon's personal million. Actually, Sam's share of the check was exactly nil; throughout his tenure as airport manager he had been on a straight salary basis and had no stock in the airport corporation.

With receipt of the million-dollar check, Sam Solomon closed out a chapter of his business career. After more than eight years of living a hectic double life, Sam was at last a normal human with only one full-time job, as president of Northeast Airlines. Well, almost normal; his home was in Maryland and his job in New England, and he refused to change either, so the long-distance commuting would go on. But at least he could bring his talents into sharper focus, concentrating on the airline alone, free of the mental gear-shifting which had characterized his entire career in aviation.

He should have been delighted to lose half his burden. Somehow he was not. There was a sense of loss. The frantic happenings at Washington-Hoover, the controversy and turmoil; the battle to maintain safety against heavy odds; the continual investigations; the challanges; the frustrations; the triumphs—they all added up to one magnificent experience. Sam would remember forever the little postage-stamp airport, its people and its problems.

For the immediate future, however, Sam Solomon was to become too busy to mourn the loss. The war was now clearly visible on the horizon and there was a very large place in it for Samuel J. Solomon. Within a short time, Sam was to find himself handling not two full-time jobs, but three.

CHAPTER VII

Northeast Pioneers the North Atlantic Route

On December 8, 1941, the United States became an active belligerent in World War II. On that day, the day after Japan attacked without warning Pearl Harbor, the Philippines and Malaya, both the U.S. and the British Commonwealth formally declared war on the Japanese. Germany and Italy, Japan's Axis partners, in turn issued declarations of war against the United States.

If the way in which it came about was surprising to the American people, the fact of war was not. For months the United States had been a participant in the European war in everything but actual combat. Early in 1941, the nation had abandoned its pretense of neutrality and voted Lend-Lease aid to Britain. America's industrial arsenal was turning out millions of tons of supplies and equipment for the Allied cause and, in retaliation, German submarines were sinking American ships and disregarding stern warnings from President Roosevelt. Long before Pearl Harbor, German-American relations had been strained to the breaking point.

It is an all-but-forgotten chapter of history, but the United States actually committed armed forces to service in the North Atlantic area months before the formal declarations of war.

The fall of Denmark in 1940 had left unprotected both Greenland, a Danish territory, and Iceland, which, although technically an independent nation, looked to Denmark for guidance on foreign affairs and for defense assistance under a treaty of union. Germany, flying frequent reconnaissance flights over Greenland, left no doubt of its intentions to establish at least weather stations and possibly other bases there. It was equally clear that Iceland offered the Nazis a potentially valuable vantage point for the conduct of submarine warfare.

To forestall German occupation, Britain sent troops to Iceland in 1940. The following year, at the request of the Icelandic government, the U.S. agreed to share with Britain the responsibility for the defense of Iceland. At about the same time, the U.S. concluded an agreement with the Danish government in exile whereby the United States would undertake the defense of Greenland. In the spring and summer of 1941, the U.S. dispatched military units to "occupy" the northland countries and to survey the air base potential of Greenland and Iceland.

The original intent was to build bases for defensive purposes, but even as the surveys got under way it became apparent that the northlands offered broader utility—as links in an aerial bridge across the North Atlantic, a concept envisioned years earlier by Sam Solomon.

The British had already started to fly the North Atlantic. Rather than wait months for ship delivery of American-built aircraft, they were flying some planes across the ocean. Prior to the Lend-Lease Act, when the U.S. was still paying lip service to its posture of neutrality, the aircraft were delivered to points on the U.S. side of the Canadian border, then rolled across the international line. By this device, the U.S. technically avoided the hostile act of flying combat aircraft directly to a belligerent dominion. It is doubtful whether the Germans appreciated the niceties of this disclaimer, but it satisfied the American concept of neutrality. Once in Canada, the planes were taken over by British and Canadian pilots and flown to Newfoundland, thence across the North Atlantic to Scotland.

Ocean flying, however, was restricted to the longer-ranging aircraft, medium bombers for the most part, and even these planes had to be equipped with extra fuel tanks. Smaller planes, such as light bombers and fighters, simply did not have the range for long overwater hops and they had to be transported by ship.

With the passage of the Lend-Lease Act, the flow of U.S.-built aircraft to England increased sharply, as did the British need for them. Urgency dictated that as many airplanes as possible be flown over the ocean under their own power. Thus came a plan for a new ferry route, one in which the longest overwater leg would be within the capability of most military aircraft, even fighters. From terminals in the U.S. and Canada, the route would run to Labrador, thence to Greenland and Iceland, finally to Scotland. The three overwater stages— Labrador-Greenland, Greenland-Iceland and Iceland-Scotland—would be of approximately equal lengths, each of them less than half the distance of the direct crossing from Newfoundland to Scotland.

The route, however, demanded considerable preparation. In Labrador and Greenland, there were only short strips for bush-type aircraft operations or compacted areas for ski landings on the winter snows. In Iceland, the British had built two small fields for defensive aircraft, but they were inadequate for the contemplated sustained movement of large numbers of heavy airplanes. Thus, it was necessary to construct new bases at all three northland locales. Additionally, there were requirements for weather stations and communications facilities along the route.

Development of the North Atlantic air bridge, together with an alternate route across the South Atlantic, got under way in mid-1941. At approximately the same time, the Army Air Forces created the Ferrying Command, charged with responsibility for delivering aircraft intended for Great Britain. For the most part, the planes were flown from the plants where they were built to shipping ports on the East Coast or the Gulf Coast.

In the North Atlantic area, the principal activity of the Ferrying Command was supporting development of the new far northern route, a joint United States-Canadian-British project. Sites had been selected for a number of major bases: one at Goose Bay, Labrador; one at Narsarssuak on the southern tip of Greenland; another, to serve as alternate to Narsarssuak, farther to the north on the west coast of Greenland; two more near Keflavik in Iceland. The Canadians were to handle construction at Goose Bay while the U.S. would build the other bases and the weather/communications stations. The Army Air Forces Ferrying Command was to provide logistic support for all of the installations.

Construction of the far north bases began in the fall of 1941. However, Labrador and Greenland, with shipping seasons restricted by icing to periods ranging from six months down to six weeks, were already inaccessible to surface vessels. Supplies and equipment had to be flown to the sites and ski-landed, but the Ferrying Command had only one transport available. Work progressed at an agonizingly slow pace.

The far north route was still largely a paper plan when the Japanese struck Pearl Harbor. Immediately thereafter, it was given top priority. It was no longer just an expedient for ferrying aircraft to the British. Now the United States was readying the largest aerial combat unit ever assembled—the Eighth Air Force. To be based in the British Isles, the Eighth Air Force was to team with the Royal Air Force in round-the clock-strategic bombing of Germany's industrial complex. As soon as training status would permit, hopefully in the summer of 1942, the Eighth would move to England, under its own power and across the North Atlantic route.

Some of the planes would fly the Newfoundland-Scotland route already being used by the Royal Air Force Ferry Command. The enormous amount of traffic anticipated, however, would soon saturate that route; it had become doubly imperative to develop the new Labrador-Greenland-Iceland-Scotland stepping-stone air bridge.

Thus the far northern airway had taken on multiple urgency: as a route for the Eighth Air Force; for short-range aircraft being ferried to the war theater, now American planes as well as British; and, after the Eighth Air Force was completely deployed in England, for transport airplanes bringing priority payloads, such as aircraft spare parts or replacement crews. The North Atlantic route, which Sam Solomon had once been told was of no importance to the Air Corps, had suddenly taken on tremendous significance.

* * * * * * * *

Sam Solomon, always a step or two ahead of the others, didn't wait for Pearl Harbor. Aware that the Ferrying Command was making a move in the North Atlantic, he paid a visit to command headquarters in Washington two weeks before the formal start of hostilities. There he sat down with Colonel Robert Olds, chief of the Ferrying Command, and offered him one entire airline, already operating in the northeast and experienced in cold weather flying, available immediately for whatever service the Air Corps might want to assign. Olds, who needed all the help he could get, was appreciative, but he had as yet no authority to contract with commercial carriers. He would seek such authority, he told Sam, and he would be in touch.

Sam fidgeted while waiting for Northeast's call to service. He had a strong sense of urgency and he wanted to become part of the action as quickly as possible.

The day after the Japanese attack Sam was in New York, His dual experience as airport manager and airline executive had prompted the Mayor of Los Angeles to ask him to serve on a committee. The city was planning to build a major new air terminal and was looking for just the right man to run it; it was Sam's job, along with four other committee members, to interview and screen candidates. The New York meeting, at LaGuardia Airport, was to be the first of several screening sessions at various locales.

As the committeemen introduced themselves, Sam was amazed to meet an Air Corps colonel, the commander of Hamilton Field near San Francisco.

"What are you doing here?" Sam asked him. "I should think you would be on alert status."

The colonel shrugged.

"They know where to find me."

Sam was highly incensed at the man's attitude. The Japanese had struck Hawaii only the day before and there seemed a possibility that they might follow up with an attack on the West Coast. Here was the commander of a major West Coast installation attending a meeting at the opposite end of the country, to pick a manager for an airport that would probably not get built now that war had been declared. Come to think of it, Sam asked himself, what am I doing here? He was engaged in a trivial matter at a time when he should be contributing something of importance. It was typical of Sam's feeling of urgency that he decided on the spot that this first session would be his only appearance with the screening committee.

More than a month had elapsed after Pearl Harbor before Sam got the call he had anxiously been awaiting. He was in Washington at the time, in a temporary office he had taken after the closure of Washington-Hoover Airport. The caller was Colonel Olds. Would Sam drop by Ferrying Command headquarters to discuss an assignment for Northeast Airlines?

Olds went directly to the point.

"How soon can you be ready to start service to Northwest River?" he asked.

"Tomorrow!" Sam blurted out confidently. He had never heard of Northwest River, but he assumed it was some place in Newfoundland, the logical departure point for the North Atlantic route. Since Northeast was already operating into New Brunswick, Newfoundland should pose no problem.

Get ready, Olds said, the order would come soon. For this and future missions, he added, the Ferrying Command would supply the airplanes; Northeast would be asked to provide crews, maintenance and all other operational necessities. Regrettably, a formal contract would have to wait until the command broke the logjam of paper work thrust upon it by the sudden transition to war status. In the meantime, Olds would sign a letter of intent.

Sam was willing to accept what amounted to a handshake agreement.

"If there's a job to be done, let's get it done," he said. "I'm sure someone will pay us sooner or later."

Back in his office, Sam got out his atlas and studied the Newfoundland area for Northwest River. To his surprise, he could not find it. He called Milton Anderson in Boston and asked him to check the airline's maps. Anderson called back to say that he had hunted through every Newfoundland chart and there was no trace of Northwest River.

"Well," said Sam, "we sure as hell can't fly there until we know where it is. I'll have to call Olds again." He didn't relish the idea of calling the Ferrying Command chief, who was noted for his short fuse; he felt foolish, having guaranteed to fly 'tomorrow', to a destination he knew nothing about.

"Dammit," Olds exploded, after listening to Sam's apologia, it's not in Newfoundland, it's in Labrador." Northwest River, it turned out, was another name for Goose Bay. The mission of Northeast Airlines on this first contract flight would be to deliver cargo for the support of construction and at the same time set up the airline's own station for regular service to the base.

Within a few days, the Ferrying Command delivered a transport airplane to Northeast Airlines at Boston. It was a "DC-2 1/2," a hybrid which had the smaller fuselage of the DC-2 mated to the big wing of the DC-3. Sam Solomon, on hand for the arrival, felt that the paint job—military olive drab with the starred circle of the Army Air Forces on wing and side—lacked something. He ordered the Northeast ground crew to add "Northeast Airlines" in large white lettering on the fuselage. After all, it *was* a partnership.

Late in January, with Milton Anderson personally taking command, Northeast flew its first mission in support of military operations, also the first contract flight by any commercial carrier on the North Atlantic route. Anderson and his crew departed from Boston, carrying a general cargo that included equipment for a radio station to be set up at Goose Bay. They flew via Presque Isle, Maine, one of Northeast's regular stations, to Harmon Field in Newfoundland, thence northward to Goose Bay in eastern Labrador. The crew got a taste of what it would be like to fly the North Atlantic route: there were no radio navigation aids, the weather stations being built were not yet fully operational, existing maps were unreliable and the terrain was distinctly uninviting—dense forest, rugged snow-covered mountains and hundreds of miles of muskeg, the spongy, insect-ridden bog of northern North America.

Immediately after the Goose Bay flight, Sam Solomon was again contacted by the Ferrying Command. How soon could Northeast be ready to extend service to BW-1? Sam was more cautious this time. Where, exactly, was BW-1? BW-1, it turned out, was Narsarssuak. For simplified message transmission, and for the benefit of people who could not pronounce Narsarssuak, Angmagssalik or Tunugliarfik, the Army Air Forces had assigned code names to the far north installations. Narsarssuak in southwestern Greenland became Bluie West One, or BW-1. The alternate base on the west coast of Greenland was named Bluie West Eight. The weather station at Angmagssalik on the east coast was coded Bluie East Two, and so forth.

Sam Solomon was somewhat taken aback when he learned of Northeast's destination. Bluie West One was almost 800 miles beyond Goose Bay, practically all of it over water across the Labrador Basin, a subarctic segment of the Atlantic. Northeast had practically zero experience in long overwater flights and this one was especially hazardous in light of the lack of navigational facilities. Nonetheless, Sam stated, "We'll be ready tomorrow."

The BW-1 trip was carried off successfully and followed by another extension of the route, this time to Iceland. A Northeast crew negotiated without incident the long haul from Boston through Presque Isle to Goose Bay and Bluie West One, then another 800 miles across the ocean to Meeks Field, one of two major bases the U.S. was building in Iceland.

Meanwhile, there were developments on the home front. In March, 1942, Northeast moved its pilot training school from Boston to Burlington, Vermont. There were two reasons. The first was a government edict suspending all flying, except military and airline, within 100 miles of the Atlantic coast; Boston was within the 100-mile zone, Burlington well outside it.

Additionally, however, the school had outgrown its Boston quarters. The Northeast staff now included some 30 instructors and about an equal number of technicians for maintenance of the school's 11 training planes. The average enrollment was about 80 student pilots taking advance, or "finishing school" courses which would qualify them for duty with the Ferrying Command or for service as flight instructors. Looking for a facility outside the 100-mile limit with adequate classroom space for the growing school, Solomon and Anderson found it at the University of Vermont, which made available an entire wing of a new building. Throughout the war years, the school was to turn out eight transport-rated pilots every week, a very substantial contribution to the war effort.

Sam Solomon found himself with money problems in the spring of 1942. The stock issue of 1940 had paid for the three new DC-3's and left a little for working capital, but that capital had been expended. The rising traffic volume which had dictated the need for the DC-3's unpredictably leveled off in late 1941 and dropped sharply after Pearl Harbor, when only essential travel was permitted. Although Northeast had been filling its 10-seat Electras, it could not half-fill the 24-passenger DC-3's. The number of flights was reduced, but even so the greater operating costs of the DC-3 coupled with the low level of traffic thrust the airline into a critical financial bind.

Sam lucked his way out of the dilemma. He concluded a deal with TWA in which TWA got Northeast's three almost-new DC-3's in exchange for five DC-2's, which carried only 14 passengers and would have been better for Northeast's purposes. TWA threw into the bargain $220,000 in cash, which provided Sam the operating capital he needed.

No sooner had the deal been made, however, than Northeast was ordered by the government to sell its newly-acquired DC-2's for defense purposes. With the sale money, Solomon then bought two used DC-3's from American Airlines, also at government direction.

Thus, Sam wound up the multiple transaction with nearly a quarter of a million badly-needed cash and only one fewer DC-3 than he had started with—and Northeast did not need that one anyway, in view of reduced traffic. For the remainder of the war years, the two DC-3's would handle Northeast's curtailed commercial operations, while the Army Air Forces would provide the aircraft for the company's military support effort.

In June, 1942, the Ferrying Command merged with the Air Service Command, a military transport service operating within the continental United States, and the combined organization was given a new name. To reflect the broader mission now contemplated—delivery of cargo to the war theater in addition to ferrying new aircraft—it became the Air Transport Command. Colonel Olds, meanwhile, had been succeeded by Colonel Harold L. George. George, later to become a major general, was to expand the relatively small Ferrying Command into a global Air Transport Command hauling cargoes to six continents, the greatest air freight operation in history.

That same month Northeast Airlines got the long-awaited assignment to go "all the way" across the North Atlantic. Sam was in his Washington office when a call came from Colonel Robert Love, assistant to Air Transport Command chief Hal George. The requirement, Colonel Love stated, was to fly a complete radio station over the air bridge to Stornoway, Scotland, the temporary eastern terminus of the route. American Airlines had already been contacted with regard to the assignment, but American wanted three months to survey the route and prepare pilots for that type of flying. When could Northeast be ready, the Colonel wanted to know.

"Tomorrow," Sam responded, with the remark that had become his trademark.

Half a decade after Solomon had first proposed it, Northeast would at last get its chance to fly the North Atlantic. In the process, Northeast would become the first commercial carrier ever to haul a payload over the far northern route.

Sam Solomon determined that he would go along on this flight. For one thing, he was concerned about the risky type of flying Northeast was doing in the north country, particularly the overwater missions, and he felt he could no longer send crews to places where he had not been himself. For another, it was the culmination of a dream, a momentous milestone in the history of Northeast Airlines, and Sam simply had to be aboard when the plane touched down at Stornoway. He assigned himself to the Stornoway flight over the objections of his railroad partners, who felt that plodding across the North Atlantic in a creaky, twin-engine cargo plane was too dangerous a venture for a company president.

After his conversation with Colonel Love, Sam called Milton Anderson to alert him for the mission, cleared up a few business details, then departed immediately to make sure he would catch the flight. Clad only in a tropical suit, ideal for June weather in Washington but hardly suitable for subarctic travel, he flew to Boston, then on to Presque Isle in northern Maine near the Canadian border.

Presque Isle had once been a small way station on Northeast's Boston-Portland-Bangor-Caribou run, but with America's entry into the war it had assumed great importance because of its location. Now a large and still expanding military base, it had become the main port of embarkation for aircraft flying the North Atlantic, both the direct Newfoundland-Scotland crossing or the stepping-stone route via Labrador, Greenland and Iceland. There the Air Transport Command had set up its North Atlantic Division headquarters and Northeast Airlines had created its own Military Division.

For once the military had taken Sam up on his "tomorrow" commitment. In the time it had taken him to fly from Washington, the mission had been set up and the cargo was already being loaded into a C-47, a military version of the DC-3. Sam had no time to acquire arctic flying gear; he boarded in his tropical suit.

Milton Anderson took the left-hand seat of the C-47. He was assisted by two other Northeast line captains, A. V. R. Marsh as copilot and Fred Lord as navigator. Also aboard were a radio operator, a crew chief and several radio technicians to work on installing the equipment—elements of a radio range borrowed for the duration of the war from the Milwaukee air terminal—that made up the bulk of the cargo load. The airplane was overloaded by some 5,000 pounds, a not unusual occurrence in those days of too much freight and too few airplanes to handle it. The radio equipment, in boxes and bundles, took up the entire aft and center sections of the cabin, from deck to ceiling. In the fore section were two large auxiliary fuel tanks. The passengers, including Sam Solomon, sat hunched on aluminum benches along the wall of the fuselage, with practically no leg room because of the cargo.

It was a long, monotonous flight, despite the adventure of the mission. Sam Solomon divided his time between reading and watching the bleak, rugged scenery unfold below. The difficulties of this type of flying were emphasized by the fact that, up front in the cockpit, Anderson and Lord were studying overwater navigation as they flew, reading from a book which Anderson had bought prior to departure; there were still few radio aids, and there were no familiar landmarks such as the Northeast crews used for check points on their regular commercial runs. It was strictly dead-reckoning, or mathematical navigation, using clock and compass to figure course and distance, and hoping that the wind data provided by the weather people was accurate.

Sam, feeling that he should do something useful, took over the food service chores, so the crew was treated to the spectacle of their president distributing box lunches, pouring coffee and gathering the debris. Once, when Sam was preparing to throw out some crusts after a box meal, Fred Lord tapped him on the arm and pointed below.

"If we go down out here," he shouted above the roar of the engines, "that stuff would come in mighty handy." Sam looked outside and agreed; taking the advice seriously, he stored the crusts.

The flight droned on. Goose Bay, then the overwater hop to Bluie West One at the tip of Greenland. Here, it proved, Sam was the only one properly dressed; it was one of those rare days in Greenland when the temperature hits ninety above. Sam appeared prescient as he stepped off the plane in his tropical suit while his crewmates followed in boots, sweaters and parkas.

Then the second leg, over the Greenland ice cap and the ocean to Keflavik in Iceland. Apparently Anderson and Lord had learned something from their navigation book, because they were right on target after 800 miles across the Atlantic.

As Anderson started to arrange clearance for the final leg, the Northeast Airlines station agent at Keflavik brought up a potential problem. Even in the heat of war, he said, the British were jealously guarding their prerogatives with respect to post-war commercial service across the Atlantic. They would not take kindly to the presence on board of a U.S. airline president; they would regard Solomon's trip as an effort to get a foot in the door, a quest for postwar commercial status by virtue of pioneering the route. It did not seem entirely logical to Sam, but if that was the attitude of the British he had an answer. He had, after all, been performing steward's duties on the flight, so he asked Anderson to assign him as Northeast Airlines' first steward. He was so listed on the manifest, thereby becoming an official member of the crew rather than a top-level observer. Clearance was obtained and the Northeast airplane departed on the last lap, from Keflavik to Stornoway in the Outer Hebrides Islands off the coast of Scotland.

The weather was poor at take-off from Iceland, but the meteorological people gave assurances that it would clear by the time the Northeast mission reached the Hebrides. They were wrong.

There was heavy cloud over the entire leg and Anderson descended to wave-top level to stay under the weather, flying so low that, when land was sighted, its high point was above the airplane. The C-47 touched down at Stornoway, the cargo was offloaded and a milestone flight was completed.

Sam savored the moment. He could not help recalling his long-ago argument with S. J. Hungerford, who had insisted that land-based planes could not fly the Atlantic. He remembered, too, his interview with the Assistant Chief of the Air Corps, who had stated flatly that the North Atlantic had no potential as a cargo route. Now a commercial carrier had crossed the ocean with a twin-engine land plane and, most importantly, it was Northeast Airlines which had blazed the trail. In the process, Sam Solomon had become the first airline president ever to enter a wartime combat zone.

From Stornoway, Anderson and Solomon decided, they would pay a visit to Prestwick, located on the Firth of Clyde not far from Glasgow. Northeast would be flying the northern route on a regular basis hereafter and Prestwick was to replace Stornoway as the eastern terminus as soon as work at the facility was completed, so it seemed advisable to have a familiarization look at the new installation.

To arrange clearance, Anderson, Solomon and the radio operator went to the Royal Air Force operations office at Stornoway. "Ops" happened to be in the same building as the surveillance and control center, where the RAF kept track of German submarines and aircraft operating in the North Atlantic. For that reason, it was a highly restricted area, requiring a special pass for admission. The sentry stopped the Northeast trio and demanded passes. They had none, of course. Anderson replied that the only pass he had was an old Boston-Maine railway pass but the sentry, apparently confused by the American accent, simply nodded and asked for the number. That was good enough to gain admission for the pilot and radio man, but the sentry could see no reason why the steward should be allowed in the classified facility. Sam had to wait outside.

Minus the technicians, who had stayed behind at Stornoway, the Northeast crew took off for Prestwick. They flew south along the Inner Hebrides chain and were immediately intercepted by a pair of Royal Air Force fighters. It was a tense moment, but fortunately Anderson had been briefed on the proper identification procedure; he fired a Very pistol with the proper colored flare and the fighters banked away.

At Prestwick, military security again reared its head. Although Anderson had obtained flight clearance from the Royal Air Force for the Prestwick visit, that was not good enough for the American authorities. The Northeast flight was operating under Air Transport Command orders which stated specifically that the airline was to deliver its cargo to Stornoway and return to Presque Isle; Prestwick was out of bounds to all except those who had official business there.

On landing, the Northeast plane was met by a very irate Army Air Forces colonel, the commanding officer of the base, who delivered Anderson and Solomon a loud and articulate lecture on military security in a combat zone, the classified nature of the Prestwick installation, Northeast's lack of authorization to land there and some general comments to the effect that a war lost something when civilians got involved in it. Then, having blown off the requisite steam, the colonel suddenly shifted gears. He became polite, even affable, and invited the crew on a personally-escorted sightseeing tour of the base and the surrounding area. Apparently the breach of military discipline had been forgiven.

It was time to start the stateward journey, on which, because of prevailing wind patterns over the North Atlantic, the Northeast flight could expect headwinds all the way to Presque Isle. In addition, the Scotland-Iceland leg of the trip would be considerably longer than originally planned, because the plane was departing from Prestwick rather than Stornoway. Always a careful flyer, Milton Anderson took a precautionary measure. In the cabin, which now contained only a spare engine being returned for overhaul, he installed two large drums of extra fuel, together with pumps to transfer the fuel to the auxiliary tanks already mounted in the cabin. Under normal conditions, the C-47 had sufficient range to fly any one of the legs without resort to either the auxiliary tanks or the extra drums, but it seemed advisable to take insurance against the unexpected.

The Scotland-Iceland leg was flown without incident and, after refueling, the Northeast C-47 took off from Keflavik for the second destination, Bluie West One in southern Greenland. As the plane flew over the Greenland icecap the weather took a turn for the worse; the ice continent was obscured by heavy cloud cover. By the time Anderson was ready to start the letdown for Bluie West One, the weather had deteriorated further; radio reports indicated that a storm was raging over most of southern Greenland and that ceilings and visibility were still dropping. The Northeast flight had suddenly encountered a serious problem.

Anderson called Sam Solomon to the cockpit and spelled out the difficulties. They were now flying at 10,000 feet, an altitude barely sufficient to clear the great ice cap. Their procedure would be to cross the ice cap to the southwestern edge of Greenland, then let down through the overcast. Hopefully, when they dropped beneath the cloud cover, there would be enough visibility to find the fjord which marked the gateway to Bluie West One. Then they would have to fly straight up the fjord, which was bordered on either side by towering cliffs. With low ceilings and low visibility, it would be like flying through a tunnel with no certainty that the field would be visible at the other end. Once in the tunnel, a turnaround to reverse course would be next to impossible in bad weather.

There was an alternate field at Bluie West Eight, more than 300 miles to the west, but it seemed more than a possibility that BW-8 might be similarly weatherbound. If they used an appreciable amount of fuel trying to land at either of the Greenland Bluies, there would be no other place to go if those havens were denied them. An attempt at a zero-zero landing could—most likely *would*—be fatal.

It was too late to go back to Iceland. There remained one alternative: to continue non-stop to Goose Bay, Labrador, 800 miles distant. With the fuel in the auxiliary tanks, plus that in the drums Anderson had so fortuitously provided, they could just about make it to "Goose" with perhaps a spoonful of gasoline to spare—*if* there were no further weather or mechanical emergencies.

"What do you think?" Anderson asked Sam when he had concluded his recital.

Sam shrugged.

"You don't ask a steward how to fly," he replied. "I have absolute confidence in your decision."

Anderson nodded grimly and made his choice: they would go on to Labrador.

It was a tense five hours-plus. The plane droned on across the Labrador Basin, the cockpit team anxiously watching the fuel gauges and comparing distance remaining with fuel remaining. The outlook never got better than marginal. Back in the cabin, Sam Solomon was remarkably calm. He had long ago adopted the attitude, "If you can't do anything about it, there's no point in worrying about it."

Then, with the C-47 already gobbling the reserve fuel in the extra drums, the cloud cover beneath them thinned and they could see the cold blue of the Labrador Sea, dotted by hundreds of small icebergs, and beyond, clear of cloud, the coast of Labrador. Anderson started the descent, made a normal approach and touched down gently on the Goose Bay runway. The airplane's engines gulped the last of the fuel just as the C-47 reached the parking ramp.

The first North Atlantic round trip completed, Northeast began flying the route on a regular basis. There was now a great deal of activity in the north, because the Eighth Air Force had begun its massive movement to England, flying hundreds of four-engine bombers, each carrying, in addition to the flight crew, as much of the organization's equipment and non-flying personnel as it could handle. This movement was to continue at a heavy rate through 1942 and at a somewhat reduced rate for more than two years thereafter, as replacement planes and crews supplanted some of the original force. Other airlines—notably TWA and American, flying four-engine transports—followed where Northeast had led, serving as contract carriers on the North Atlantic. There was also a considerable increase in flight frequency on the part of Air Transport Command's own military cargo craft.

In the course of supporting the North Atlantic route over a period of several months, Northeast had established its own radio navigation stations—five of them—in Newfoundland, Labrador, Greenland and Iceland. The stations, transplanted from stops on the airline's commercial routes where they were infrequently used, were invaluable assets to airmen flying the far north. Originally they were the *only* radio aids; later the Army installed several military stations.

Then, unpredictably, came an order from the Army Air Forces: Northeast must remove its radio equipment. No reason was given, but scuttlebutt had it that the Army was worried about the possibility of German submarines and aircraft homing on the stations. Scuttlebutt had no answer for the obvious question: even if Northeast removed the equipment, why couldn't the Germans home on the military stations? It was one of those frustrating orders, so often issued in the war years, that gave rise to the satirical saying, "There's no reason for it, dammit, it's just policy."

The Northeast flight crews didn't like the order a bit; there were still precious few navaids in the north and the removal of any one of them increased the hazard of northland flying. From his own experience, Sam Solomon could sympathize with their point of view. Forget it, he told Anderson, let's pretend we didn't get the word.

It didn't work. Solomon was summoned to Washington, to the office of Colonel Si Marriner, chief of communications of the Army Air Forces. Northeast had been given an order to remove the stations, Marriner said. They had not been removed. They must be removed immediately.

Sam argued. "Those stations are the best navigation and communication system in the North Atlantic."

They had, Marriner admitted, proved a valuable adjunct. "Nonetheless," he added, "my orders are to remove them."

"Who can change those orders?" Sam asked.

"One of two people."

"Who are they? I'll go see them."

"President Roosevelt and Winston Churchill," said Marriner.

"All right," Sam conceded, "I give up." Reluctantly, he passed on the order to dismantle the stations.

By late 1942, Northeast was flying seven aircraft over its military routes, most of them C-47's and the others Curtiss C-46's, huge, fat-bellied, twin-engine transports capable of carrying considerably more cargo than the C-47's.

The military route structure had expanded enormously, to the point where it was many times larger than Northeast's combined commercial routes. A major factor in Northeast's expansion of service to the military was the creation of another new route by means of which airplanes could be ferried from the West Coast of the United States through central Canada, across Hudson Bay and the Northwest territories to Greenland, where the new inland route merged with the standard far north route to Scotland. Maintenance of this route demanded a number of new weather and communications stations which had to be air-supported as well as the ferry bases.

In addition to regular service from Presque Isle to Scotland, Northeast Airlines was occasionally flying a mid-Atlantic route to England via the Azores. The airline was also making regular or special runs to Newfoundland; northern Quebec; Labrador; Baffin Island, north of Labrador; to the weather stations in the Baffin-Greenland area; far to the west, to Winnipeg and Churchill in Manitoba; to Southampton Island, north of Hudson Bay; and to remote outposts far above the Arctic Circle. It was a mammoth route structure totaling some 10,000 miles and the assignment frequency was such that the airline's seven planes were in constant use.

Much of the flying was routine delivery of supplies and equipment, but there were frequent special missions of an even more hazardous nature. Once Northeast was called upon to fly to Hebron, a tiny Eskimo village in eastern Labrador where the Army Air Forces had a weather station. It was an emergency mission, to bring out the station's cook, stricken by appendicitis. The Northeast pilot made a wheeled landing on compacted snow, but the wheels broke through the crust and buried in the soft snow beneath. The pilot mustered the entire Eskimo population to dig out the airplane, then made a risky take-off in dense fog in order to get the cook to medical attention in time.

On another occasion, Northeast participated in a combat mission of sorts. A crew heading for Greenland sighted a surfaced submarine, believed to be German, lying at rest off the Greenland coast. The navigator carefully fixed the sub's position and reported it on arrival at the base. The base commander had apparently been fighting off the arctic boredom by dipping into the medicinal brandy. Excitedly, he attached the Northeast plane and crew to his command, loaded aboard a depth charge and went after the submarine.

It was fortunate that the Germans had vacated the premises in the interim, for the slow-moving C-47 would have been a sitting duck for the U-boat's deck guns.

The two pilots who had flown with Anderson and Solomon on the first transatlantic crossing—A. V. R. Marsh and Fred Lord—figured prominently in Northeast's most dramatic wartime missions.

Lord was the leader of a heroic rescue operation in February, 1943. A four-engine C-87 transport, flown by an American Airlines crew headed by Captain Owen J. "Buck" O'Connor and carrying 17 passengers, made a forced landing in northern Quebec. The plane landed on a frozen lake and buried waist-deep in the soft snow covering the thick ice.

For several days Army Air Forces and contract carrier aircraft searched the area of O'Connor's last known position. Once the downed plane was sighted briefly, but weather obscured it before a positive fix could be obtained.

On the morning of the sixth day, Fred Lord led a five-plane search-and-rescue mission, bringing with him in the lead plane an Army arctic explorer, Colonel Hubbard, to serve as on-the-spot survival expert should the O'Connor group be sighted.

Five hours into the search, an American Airlines crew commanded by Ernest Gann, later to become a best-selling novelist, found O'Connor. Gann parachuted supplies and reported the position of the downed airplane to Lord, who immediately flew to the area and air-dropped his own cargo.

Lord then consulted with Colonel Hubbard as to whether he should try to land. Lord's C-47 was not ski-equipped and it would probably bury in the snow as had O'Connor's plane. But O'Connor's crew and passengers had spent almost a week on the ice lake and might be too weak to help themselves. Lord's healthy five-man crew, which included the arctic survival expert, could provide invaluable assistance and Lord's aircraft radio would allow contact with other rescuers. Fully aware that he was stranding himself and his crew, Lord proceeded to land the C-47 on "Lake O'Connor."

Supplied by air drop when rescue planes could penetrate the tough winter weather, the Lord-O'Connor team worked for 16 arduous days, in temperatures ranging from zero to minus 30, to dig a runway. Incredibly, against tremendous odds, the group managed to clear a 1200-foot ice strip, enabling both airplanes to fly out.

Only a month later, March and an all-volunteer crew displayed similar courage on a rescue/supply mission. At Arctic Bay, a tiny weather outpost far north of the Arctic Circle, a meteorologist needed immediate medical attention. In addition, Arctic Bay and Fort Ross, another weather station about 300 miles to the west, were icebound and the surface supply vessel had been unable to reach them for more than a year; both bases were desperately short of supplies.

Neither station had a runway. Both were north of the north magnetic pole, the deepest arctic penetration ever attempted by a contract carrier. In addition to the weather difficulties, the airplane compass would be useless because of polar magnetism. Marsh would have to navigate primarily by sun sightings, when and if the sun was visible.

Marsh somehow found Arctic Bay, managed a rough landing on the snow-topped ice, then taxied back and forth several times, creating deep ruts which would serve as a take-off runway. On the first flight, he brought in some supplies and flew out the ill weather man. Two more flights were needed to haul additional supplies to the two outposts. For this extremely risky operation, Marsh and his fellow airmen were awarded Air Medals, an honor rarely accorded an airline crew.

Northeast Airlines' performance in support of the North Atlantic route was a magnificent one, accomplished under extraordinarily difficult conditions, and despite those conditions, without a fatality. It was professional flying at its best. It was a war contribution as important in its way as that of the men who were bombing Germany. No one was prouder than Sam Solomon, not for himself, but for his Northeast people and the way they had executed his commitment to the war effort.

CHAPTER VIII

Solomon and the Airlines War Training Institute

While Northeast Airlines' flight crews continued to ply the arctic routes, their president found himself with a new job. Not a different job, but *another* job in addition to his duties as president of the airline. After less than a year's respite as a single-occupation man, Sam Solomon resumed the double-duty existence that he had thought ended with the closure of Washington-Hoover Airport. This time the additional job was one of the most important in a nation at war, that of directing the training of flight and ground crews for the rapidly expanding Air Transport Command.

It happened in mid-1942 and it stemmed from the fact that ATC was having trouble finding enough people to man its growing fleet. The Command's initial problem, in the early months after America's entry into the war, had been an insufficiency of transport aircraft. That problem was being solved. It had taken the American industrial arsenal some time to swing into high gear, but now aircraft manufacturers were turning out planes by the thousands. In the transport category, they were building twin-engine Douglas C-47's, the new four-engine Douglas C-54 heavy transport and another four-engine craft, the Consolidated Vultee C-87, a cargo modification of a heavy bomber; soon to start rolling off the production line was another twin-engine craft, the Curtiss C-46. At the time of Pearl Harbor, transport output had amounted only to a trickle; now it had grown to a steady stream and within a year it would become a torrential flow of hundreds of new airplanes every month.

With every passing day, Air Transport Command was expanding its global route structure and flight frequencies in support of mounting deployment of Allied combat units all over the world. In addition to the North Atlantic route to Scotland and England, ATC was flying a Mid-Atlantic route through the Azores; over the South Atlantic to North Africa; across north central Africa to India, Burma and China; island-hopping the Pacific to Australia; and through northwest Canada to Alaska.

To meet these commitments, ATC had mustered all the available military personnel trained in transport operations. It had leaned heavily on the airlines, who were now flying about half of all cargoes lifted. The Command had similarly drawn upon the graduates of the Civilian Pilot Training Program. But these reservoirs of civilian talent were drying up and there was a critical need for more—a great many more—transport personnel of all types: pilots, navigators, radio operators, flight engineers, flight controllers, mechanics and a variety of other ground occupations.

In July, 1942, all of the presidents of the airlines engaged in ATC activities were summoned to a Washington meeting by Major General Harold L. George, commanding general of Air Transport Command. As president of Northeast, Sam Solomon joined the group at the Carlton Hotel. It was an illustrious gathering, including the chief executives of all the major airlines and many of the smaller carriers. Nineteen companies were represented, most of them already performing contract haulage for ATC, a few of them also training transport personnel in schools like the one Northeast was operating at Burlington.

General George addressed the group. The U.S. airlines had responded magnificently, he said, to the War Department's initial call for assistance, both in contract transport and in the training operation. Now the War Department was asking the airlines to join in a broader effort. The Army could take fresh recruits and provide them basic training in either flight or ground skills. The Army, however, had neither the facilities nor the experience necessary to handle the advanced phases of the training program, the "finishing school" development of thoroughly qualified transport personnel. That job must be assumed by the airlines.

This would mean, George continued, expansion of the existing airline schools and creation of many new ones to accommodate the heavy flow of trainees anticipated. Additionally, the scope of the instruction programs must be broadened to include a number of new courses. The courses had to be time-compressed without sacrifice of quality. Textbooks and training manuals had to be created. Most of all, said the ATC commander, the training must be conducted on a unified basis, under the aegis of a central organization which would be simultaneously a liaison group between ATC and the individual airlines and a management group to oversee the program.

Captain Eddie Rickenbacker, president of Eastern Air Lines, took the floor to assure General George of the airlines' solid support. As for the proposed central organization, he added, it could only be as good as the man selected to head it. In his view, there was one man outstandingly qualified for the job: Samuel J. Solomon, whose Northeast Airlines had led the way in the establishment of airline training schools and whose Burlington institution was exemplary of the professional standards ATC sought. The other airline presidents agreed; they unanimously backed the nomination.

Sam Solomon had listened to Rickenbacker in amazement. He had encountered Rickenbacker on a number of occasions since their hot dispute in Washington-Hoover Airport days and their relations had been neither cordial nor hostile. Sam had always felt that Rickenbacker harbored some resentment, because it was known in the industry that when "Cap'n Eddie" got mad he stayed mad. Now his former antagonist was nominating him, Sam Solomon, for one of the most important posts in the war effort.

Caught unprepared, Sam stood up slowly, conflicting thoughts running through his mind. His proposed assignment was undeniably an important one. It offered an opportunity to contribute in even greater measure to the war effort, and that was the paramount consideration to Sam Solomon. But how would Alma react to the idea of renewed double duty? What would be the attitude of the Northeast Airlines board? Could he handle the new job without diluting his value to Northeast? And to what extent could he count on airline and ATC support?

"I'm flattered by your confidence," he told the group, "and I would like very much to accept this assignment. But I can't give you a yes or no at this moment. Let me sleep on it and I'll advise you tomorrow."

Alma Solomon felt that perhaps Sam was taking on too heavy a load, but she recognized the intensity of his feeling about war service; if Sam felt that he should undertake the training job, then that was the way it should be. Northeast's board similarly acquiesced. Sam then paid a visit to ATC headquarters at Gravelly Point, adjacent to Washington National Airport, and sought out Cyrus Rowlett Smith. "C.R.", as Smith was known throughout the industry, was president-on-leave of American Airlines, doing wartime duty as chief of staff of ATC with the rank of brigadier general.

He could only be effective in the training post if he had the solid backing of both the airlines and the ATC staff, Sam told Smith. How about it? C.R. dropped a hint that airline support might be harder to come by than military cooperation.

"I want to remind you of one thing," he said. "The airline presidents individually are nice guys, but collectively they're a bunch of terrible people."

"You ought to know, C.R.," Sam replied with a grin.

"So should you, you're one of them," Smith said. As for himself and the ATC staff, he added, Sam could count on complete cooperation. As things turned out later, Sam did get full support from Smith and the Command throughout the life of the program.

So assured, Sam met with the airline presidents the following day and announced that he would accept the assignment if each of the airlines would pledge total support. The airline presidents responded with promises of technical personnel to staff the central organization and whatever other help Sam needed. Many—but not all— kept their promises.

Having taken the plunge, Solomon's first thought was of a top-level assistant to share the workload. A name jumped to mind: Jerome Lederer, the chief of the Safety Bureau of the Civil Aeronautics Board, whom Sam had known for some time. Lederer's background in air safety, with the CAB and earlier with an insurance underwriting firm, would effectively complement Sam's own organizational and leadership talents. A tireless and efficient worker, Lederer also shared Sam's sense of urgency about the war.

Sam arranged a meeting and outlined the program to Lederer, who was instantly enthusiastic.

"I'll go back and resign from the CAB right now," he told Sam.

"Wait a minute," said Solomon. "It's only tentative. We have no contract, no appropriation, no money to pay anyone. Wait until the War Department and the airlines iron out the status of this project."

Lederer couldn't wait. Only a half-hour after he left the meeting, Sam received a call from L. Welch Pogue, chairman of the Civil Aeronautics Board. Pogue was unhappy about what he called a "dirty trick."

"Jerry Lederer just came in and resigned," the chairman snapped. "He said he was working for you."

Sam pleaded only partially guilty, admitting he had sounded out Lederer but had made no commitment. Pogue was somewhat appeased. "That sounds like Jerry," the board chairman said. "When he gets enthused about a new project he has to start moving on it right this minute."

"He's a man after my own heart," Sam commented.

On August 11, 1942, the training program went into operation under the designation Airlines War Training Institute, an unincorporated association composed of 19 U.S. airlines. Sam Solomon was named president and director of training; Lederer became vice president. The Army Air Forces was to fund the cost of training and AWTI's overhead, and additionally to provide a nominal fee, the purpose of which was to cover items of expenditure disallowed by the AAF's sometimes overzealous bookkeepers. Air Transport Command was to recruit personnel among the graduates of the AAF's basic training program. It was to channel them, through AWTI, into the airline-operated training facilities, including a great many new schools being created especially for this project.

Sam set up the main office of AWTI in Washington, and, for purposes of coordinating with ATC's Domestic Transportation Division, another office in New York. The Domestic Transportation Division, AWTI's military overseer, was located in a block-long edifice which fronted on both Pine and Wall Streets. The official address was 40 Wall Street, but in one of those nonsensical decisions which characterized the military's wartime public relations effort, Domestic Transportation Division chose to use the 33 Pine Street address; it would be bad for the AAF image, some dullwit thought, to have an address among the capitalists of Wall Street.

Sam Solomon was having none of that. He had "40 Wall Street" printed on his letterhead, an action which drew remonstrance from AAF officers; AWTI should properly use the same address as Domestic Transportation Division, they told Sam. "Listen," Solomon snorted, "I've been waiting all my life for an office on Wall Street and you're not going to make me use the back door."

The AWTI program was barely under way when Sam had a visit from Orval "Red" Mosier, senior vice president of American Airlines. American had been one of the first airlines to start a transport training school and Mosier apparently felt that his company had the greatest experience in that line, notwithstanding the fact that Sam's Northeast Airlines had been *the* first in the field. Mosier laid down the law:

"We're going to tell you how to run this training program."

"Red," said Solomon, "I was under the impression that I was running this program—with assistance from the airlines, of course, but not direction."

"We're going to tell you," Mosier insisted. "If you don't do it our way, American will withdraw from the program."

"All right," Sam said agreeably, reaching for the phone.

"Who are you calling?" Mosier asked.

"I'm calling General George to inform him that American is getting out of the program."

Mosier backed down quickly, "Wait a minute," he surrendered. "Let's talk this over some more." That was the last time Sam encountered interference from any airline.

With some personnel supplied by the airlines and others recruited by Solomon, the AWTI headquarters staff in Washington grew to a total of 45 people within a few months and remained at about that level. The key people, in addition to Sam and Lederer, were Clarence Belinn, the maintenance specialist who had teamed with Sam in the creation of Boston-Maine Airways; Austin Naylor, a former government employe who took over the office of treasurer; and Ruth Basius, Sam's secretary at Northeast's Boston office, who came to Washington for two weeks to help get things organized and never got back to Boston.

The AWTI headquarters staff had two primary functions. First it served as a liaison group between Air Transport Command and the 19 member airlines, freeing ATC of the necessity of dealing individually with each of the airline-operated schools. The airlines channeled through AWTI a wide range of inquiries, from requests for basic policy decisions to be determined by the Army Air Forces, to detailed questions regarding government regulations. Operating in the other direction, AWTI maintained close contact with ATC with regard to contemplated increases in the number of trainees assigned, changes in curricula and new types of equipment required. In this manner, AWTI was able to advise each member airline well in advance as to future requirements for housing, equipment and instruction. AWTI also served as clearing house for acquisition of training aids, enabling the Army Air Forces to take advantage of the economies of group purchasing and at the same time assuring uniformity of equipment in the training program.

AWTI's other major function, and the most important one, was supervision of the training work being performed by the many different airlines. It was essential to Air Transport Command that the students not only receive high-caliber instruction but also that the same procedures and techniques were taught in each of the multiple training categories—pilot, navigator, mechanic, etc. To that end, Solomon, Lederer and others of the headquarters staff traveled endlessly, to all of the more than 100 separate facilities under AWTI's direction. They checked the quality of instruction, methods of examination, and adequacy of equipment, and they took steps to bring about conformity when one unit was found to be out of line with the general standard.

One of AWTI's most valuable contributions was the preparation of training manuals, which were practically non-existent in 1942. Sam Solomon personally took over supervision of this facet of AWTI's work, because he had some very definite ideas on how to hammer home to new flyers the lessons learned from long experience of others.

"I remember sweating over dull, unimaginative textbooks in school," he told a Washington reporter. "I decided that if we expect these boys to learn in a hurry we have to give them books that they'll read with some interest. So I operate on the theory that our books be so written that flying students, or anyone else for that matter, will actually *want* to read them."

Following up on the theory, Sam dictated that the books be written very simply, free of the customary military gobbledeygook, that they be printed in large type and illustrated by clever cartoons. An example of the simplicity of style was the opening line of a manual called Survival, which in 116 brief pages contained an encyclopedia's worth of fact on how to stay alive when forced down in the ocean, the arctic, the jungle or the desert: "The aim of this book is to get you out of a jam almost anywhere. But we can't help you if you don't help yourself."

To get the book program off the ground without waiting for government appropriations to come through, Sam and Alma Solomon personally advanced the funding for initial expenses. For informational input, AWTI drew upon the combined experience of its 19 member airlines, other privately-operated schools engaged in the Civilian Pilot Training Program, and government agencies such as the Office of Education. Part-time writers were hired from airline and aviation magazine sources. Starting in late 1942, AWTI published 28 manuals in less than a year. In addition to *Survival*, exemplary titles included *Pilot's Technical Manual*, *Instructor's Manual*, *Flight Principles*, *Navigation Principles*, *Weather Principles*, and *Use of Numbers*, the latter an exercise in reasoning problems.

The books were distributed free of charge, and in quantities of hundreds of thousands, to the airline schools; to ATC, for use by its crews and passengers; and to anyone else, within or without the military establishment who had need of them. They met with tremendous acclaim from both the War and Navy Departments and from government and civilian aviation interests. Typical of the comments was this from veteran airline pilot Captain Fred Smith, writing in the U.S. Air Services magazine: "If a man could read and digest all the material in these textbooks, he'd *really* know his stuff. I can't recall a more sane and efficient treatment of the problems that present themselves to a pilot."

For Sam Solomon, it was a hectic, wearing, but nonetheless satisfying period. He spent a good part of his time in the Washington headquarters, but necessity dictated frequent trips to the New York AWTI office. In addition, he personally inspected many of the airline-operated training facilities scattered throughout the country. At the same time, he never slighted his responsibilities as president of Northeast Airlines. He continued to commute to Boston, as he had before, but he was also required to visit on occasion the airline's Military Division at Presque Isle. The pace of his earlier dual existence, in Washington-Hoover Airport days, now seemed almost leisurely by comparison.

By the fall of 1943, 14 months after the start of the program, AWTI was a going concern operating as smoothly as if it had been in business for a decade. The airline schools efficiently absorbed increases in student assignees and changes in curricula, and they maintained throughout the program an instructional standard with which Air Transport Command was more than pleased. Even more impressive was the manner in which the schools adapted to the urgency of the need and compressed training times. Courses which in peacetime had taken a year to two years to complete were cut to 60 and 90 days. AWTI schools benefited, of course, from the fact that their students had already completed some form of basic training, but even so the training time reduction was all but incredible.

Sam Solomon disclaimed credit for AWTI's brilliant wartime performance, passing the plaudits to Lederer and others. They had, in fact, done a remarkable job but the tremendous organizational effort bore the unmistakable imprint of Sam Solomon. The Washington Post took note of that fact: "The rapidity with which the program got under way is in large part due to the imaginative Mr. Solomon. He has a record of getting things done in a hurry, with a minimum of detail and a maximum of efficiency."

In September, 1943, the Army Air Forces decided that AWTI had completed its assignment. In 14 months the airline schools had turned out some 12,000 flight crew members and about 35,000 ground personnel in a number of different categories. The expansion of the Air Transport Command fleet was virtually completed and, since ATC did not have to contend with combat losses, it had been able to build up a force of trained airmen and technicians adequate for its needs. There would, of course, be continuing requirements for replacement personnel, due to attrition by aircraft accidents or normal rotation policies. These replacements would be trained in the airline schools, but the rate of output would be considerably lower. With the bulk of the training effort accomplished, ATC felt that its own staff could handle the supervisory and coordinating functions performed until now by AWTI. Accordingly, the Command issued an order disbanding Solomon's institute as of October 31, 1943.

Sam Solomon closed down his Washington and New York offices. Some of the AWTI staff joined ATC, others returned to the airlines from which they had come. Publishing rights for the training manuals were assigned to the Infantry Journal. Making a final audit, Sam found that AWTI had a moderate cash surplus. He turned the money over to the Army Air Forces Aid Society, for which he received a letter of appreciation from General H. H. "Hap" Arnold, the commanding general of the AAF.

From ATC's Domestic Transportation Division, Sam received a commendation for a job well done. Wrote Colonel Harold R. Harris, commanding officer of the Division: "Your tireless energy and self-sacrificing motives in accomplishing so successfully the task assigned have earned for you the gratitude of the Army Air Forces and the respect and admiration of the officers of this Division with whom you have worked so faithfully."

The airlines also rewarded Sam for an outstanding job by presenting him a silver tray, engraved "For his contributions to our country's war effort." It was signed by all of the presidents of the participating airlines. All but one—there was no signature from Northeast Airlines, because Sam would not permit his own company to be a party to a gift to himself.

The exigencies of war delayed a more formal expression of government recognition, but in July, 1947, Sam Solomon belatedly received, from President Harry S. Truman, a Certificate of Merit for a major contribution to America's air mobilization.

The shutdown of AWTI did not exactly leave Sam with time on his hands. The Northeast presidency alone would have kept him fully occupied, but, just as AWTI reached its peak, Sam had been tapped for still another major assignment. Incredibly, for a period of five months in 1943 Sam Solomon held down three distinctly separate jobs, any one of which could have been considered full-time employment.

CHAPTER IX

A Meeting with President Roosevelt

Except for his initial experience with the government, Sam Solomon never had to go looking for a job. Rather, it seemed, jobs came looking for him. To paraphrase an old adage, if you build a better image than the next man, the world will beat a path to your door.

So it happened that in mid-1943 Sam found himself engaged not in the customary two simuljobs, but in three.

The third assignment originated with the interest of Army Air Forces chief General Hap Arnold in the future of civil aviation. A man of long-ranging view, Arnold was already looking ahead toward the postwar transition to normalcy. As a military man, Arnold would have no peacetime jurisdiction over commercial operations, but as wartime overseer of the mobilized airlines he felt a responsibility to plan in advance for a smooth changeover once hostilities ended.

In June, 1943, General Arnold sent telegrams to the presidents of all the airlines operating outside the United States in support of the Air Transport Command commanding their presence at a meeting in his Pentagon office the following day. Sam Solomon was in Boston at the time, busy on Northeast Airlines matters, but when one received an order from Hap Arnold, one immediately dropped everything else and hastened to comply. Sam flew back to Washington.

The next day, wearing his Airlines War Training Institute badge Number One as an aid to clearing the Pentagon's tight security, Sam drove from his Silver Spring home, through Washington and across the ancient Highway Bridge over the Potomac. The scene was familiar and yet unfamiliar. The approaches to the Pentagon took him through what had once been Washington-Hoover Airport, although there were visible no traces of his former domain. A half-mile to the west, on what had once been open ground, was the enormous Pentagon, the largest office building in the world, a 34-acre mass of concrete housing the brain center of America's military operations.

In an anteroom of Arnold's Pentagon suite, Sam met with the other airline presidents, and the group was ushered into the general's personal office.

Arnold, never one to waste a word, came quickly to the point. The airlines represented at the meeting, most of which had been providing only domestic service before the war, were now flying routes all over the world. They were demonstrating the postwar potential of passenger travel over those routes—but who would fly those future routes? It was time to start thinking about it, Arnold said, and to develop an attitude, lest the United States be caught at war's end unprepared as regards aviation policy. What he wanted from the airlines, the general concluded, was a statement of their consensus as to future worldwide aviation policy.

Responding for the group, Sam Solomon said they would begin work on a policy statement immediately. Arnold stood up, indicating that the meeting was terminated, and started to summon an escort to guide the aviation people out of the Pentagon, a wartime security requirement. Then he noticed Solomon's badge.

"Sam," he said, "you won't need an escort. Will you take these gentlemen down?"

Sam accepted the assignment proudly and stepped off with assurance like an old Pentagon hand, which he was not; he had only the barest acquaintance with the huge "Puzzle Palace." The Pentagon's bewildering maze of rings, corridors and sub-corridors soon defeated him, as it had bested many a visitor; he became lost. With a squad of presidents trailing him, Sam desperately groped for an exit and, after an interminable walk, found one. It was the wrong one, he discovered, since there was no sign of his car. The group broke up, agreeing to meet at the Carlton Hotel, and Sam embarrassedly started a search for his auto.

At the Carlton meeting, the presidents conducted a post-mortem of the Arnold session and launched the Airlines Committee for United States Air Policy, charged with drafting the statement General Arnold wanted. Since he was already serving as the airlines' military liaison man in his AWTI capacity, Sam Solomon was a logical choice for a committee assignment. To round out the committee, the presidential group selected Jack Frye, president of TWA; Croil Hunter, president of Northwest Airlines; C. Bedell Munro, president of Pennsylvania Central Airlines; and Paul Brattain, vice president of Eastern Air Lines. Sam Solomon and Bob Thach, Washington representative for Northwest Airlines, were to serve as the principal architects of the policy statement draft. It was also decided, since every airline harbored ambitions to fly overseas in the postwar period, that the group should be expanded to include all U.S. airlines, not just those already flying outside the U.S.

Although the group did not formally designate a chairman at this state of the assignment, Sam Solomon, as a Washington man familiar with the workings of the government, was regarded as the committee spearhead. He was directed to set up a new office in Washington for the policy committee. His existing AWTI office would not do, it was felt, because there should be no overlap between the two airline partnerships.

So Sam rented a suite in the Carlton as policy committee headquarters. Thus, in addition to his long-range commuting between Washington, New York, Boston, Presque Isle and the AWTI-supervised schools around the country, Sam now started a short-range commuting program. Daily he walked the six blocks between the Carlton and his AWTI headquarters in the YMCA building. On a number of occasions he noticed an oddity. When he walked through Lafayette Park, across from the White House, there was elder statesman Bernard Baruch seated on a park bench. When Sam made the return trip, Baruch was still there—but at a different bench. Sam puzzled over this and finally concluded that the old gentleman was not giving equal time to the various benches, merely following the sun.

Although committees in general are rarely noted for prompt, decisive action, the airlines policy committee moved swiftly, hammering out a draft statement in day and night sessions in the Carlton suite. It was important work. Never before had there been an enunciation of policy regarding overseas flight of U.S. carriers, principally because there had been so little international activity in the pre-war years. The statement being forged by the team would represent the consensus attitude of the nation's airlines, and hopefully it would provide the foundation for a formal declaration of national policy. Hence the committee's conclusions would have sweeping implications for the future of commercial aviation, affecting foreign carriers as well as American airlines.

There was naturally some divergence of opinion as to who should be allowed to fly where, but on one major point there was unanimity: all commercial aviation should be privately-owned and operated. There were frequent rumors—not entirely unfounded—that the United States might follow the lead of European nations and create a single, government-owned airline to handle all overseas traffic. The committee had to go on record against that possibility.

One school of thought, led by Pan American Airways' Juan Trippe, held the view that a single privately-owned airline should be designated to carry the American flag abroad, a "chosen instrument" of American air commerce. Pan Am officials naturally felt that they had prior claim to such designation, by virtue of the fact that Pan Am was the first U.S. international carrier and that it was not permitted to operate domestically. Aware that the chosen instrument idea would find little sympathy in the policy group, Trippe withdrew from the committee at the outset of deliberations.

A variation of the chosen instrument theme was the idea, espoused by United Air Lines' W. A. Patterson among others, that there should be a joint international airline company composed of a number of autonomous divisions, each assigned a separate route structure. All airlines would be allowed to invest in the company but flying participation would be limited to those carriers with substantial overseas experience. Patterson disavowed interest in overseas routes and, although he did not formally withdraw from the committee, his United Air Lines people did not participate actively in the policy drafting.

Majority opinion believed that there should be "free and open" competition for overseas routes. However, the committee recognized the need for some degree of control, for overcompetition—too many airlines competing for passengers on the same route—would be economically disastrous.

Within a few weeks, the committee completed a draft statement and circulated it among the nation's major airlines for ratification. Sixteen airlines signed. Pan American, as expected, withheld its approval. So did American Export Airlines, another international carrier, on the original go-round; Export, however, later came around to the consensus view. United Air Lines wavered from one side to the other; UAL's president W. A. Patterson signed the document, then withdrew the sanction.

On July 8, Sam Solomon went to General Arnold and outlined the committee's findings and on July 15 the group held a well-attended press conference in the Carlton's banquet hall. By tacit agreement, or perhaps, as he said, because he was "first down the steps" of the banquet hall, Sam inherited the spokesman's job. To the large gathering of newsmen, he delivered the substance of the airlines' policy statement:

"I. Free and open competition—world-wide—subject to reasonable regulation by the appropriate government agencies.

"II. Private ownership and management.

"III. Fostering and encouraging by the government of the United States of a sound world-wide air transportation system.

"IV. Freedom of transit in peaceful flight—world-wide.

"V. Acquisition of civil and commercial outlets required in the public interest."

Clarified, the statement meant that there should be no monopoly by either a government-owned or a privately-owned chosen instrument and that all airlines should be permitted to bid for overseas routes. To preclude overcompetition, the President of the United States, after studying recommendations of the Civil Aeronautics

Board, would decide who would get what route; this was simply a reaffirmation of a provision of the original Civil Aeronautics Act of 1938.

The committee proposed a U.S. air transportation network extending to just about every civilized area of the globe, and further proposed the concept of "innocent flight," the right of one nation's civil aircraft to overfly the airspace of another. The committee recognized that the U.S. government would have to negotiate landing rights in foreign countries and that acquisition of these rights would entail reciprocal agreements whereby foreign carriers would be permitted to fly passengers to, and board passengers from, terminals in the United States. Finally, the committee suggested, the air bases and navigational facilities built all over the world at the expense of the American taxpayer should be made available to both American and foreign airlines when they had served the military purposes for which they had been built.

At a meeting following the press conference, the airline group formally elected Sam Solomon chairman of the policy committee. Sam never thought of demurring, although he was already totally occupied with his Northeast and AWTI jobs; after all, it was another big challenge and he felt flattered that the president of a small airline should be called upon to lead the giants of the industry, "a very tiny tail wagging a great big dog," as he put it. Moreover, the committee had quasi-military status, since it had been convened at General Arnold's request, and in wartime one could not turn down what was in effect another military assignment.

Seeking the support of the President of the United States—Franklin D. Roosevelt—for the statement of policy, Chairman Solomon requested an appointment and received one for August 6. Sam was overwhelmed by the prospect of sitting down with the President; despite his own considerable rank and stature, he still had the man-in-the-street's awe of great authority and celebrity, particularly for Roosevelt, who unquestionably ranked as the most important man in the world. Sam couldn't sleep the night before the interview; he tossed and turned all night, mentally reviewing and revising the persuasive arguments he would thrust upon the President.

The next morning he donned his best suit, stopped at the Carlton for a haircut and a shoeshine, then walked the three blocks to the White House. At the main entrance of the Executive Mansion, he was met by a Presidential assistant and escorted to an anteroom of Roosevelt's office. There he was greeted by Major General "Pa" Watson, the President's aide.

“We’re running a little late,” Watson apologized. “There’s one ahead of you. This man—” Watson jerked his head contemptuously in the direction of a little man nervously clutching a portfolio—“has some stamps to give the President.” The little man proved to be the Minister from Luxembourg.

Watson repeatedly opened the door of the President’s inner office a trifle, peered in and checked his watch. Apparently the President’s visitor—a British diplomat, as it turned out—was overstaying his appointed time. “Damned English,” Watson muttered. Finally the Briton departed, by another door as was the custom, and Watson, checking, turned to the Luxembourger.

“All right, Mr. Minister, you have exactly 30 seconds.”

The minister leaped to his feet and darted into the inner office as though Watson were holding a stop-watch. He obviously heeded the warning, for in a surprisingly short time Watson beckoned Sam to enter the President’s chamber.

Behind the massive desk in the Oval Office was the face Sam had seen a thousand times in photographs—the large silver-topped head, the rimless pince-nez, the broad toothy smile of welcome. Sam’s feeling of awe mounted. The President waved Sam to a seat near his desk.

“Sam, I’m certainly glad to meet you,” boomed the familiar deep voice. Roosevelt tapped the stamps on his desk and held up the presentation note that had accompanied them, signed by the Grand Duchess of Luxembourg. “Isn’t this the sweetest thing you ever heard?” he asked. “It says ‘From your smallest ally.’”

The President reached for his famous long-stemmed cigarette holder and offered Sam a cigarette from his pack.

“No thank you, Mr. President, I don’t smoke,” Sam said. That, he reflected later, was about the most intelligible sentence he uttered in the course of the meeting. He handed the President a copy of the policy statement, together with a volume of *Survival*, the best-selling manual published by Sam’s Airlines War Training Institute, blurting out something incoherent about the nature of his offerings. The smooth phrases of appeal over which he had labored through a sleepless night vanished into a dim recess of his mind.

The President glanced briefly at book and statement, then launched into one of the rambling monologues for which he was noted. Visitors would find, Eleanor Roosevelt wrote later, “that the questions they wanted to ask, or the opinion they wanted to state, never got into words because Franklin talked so steadily and so interestingly that they forgot what they had come to say.”

“I’m way ahead of you fellows in aviation,” the President began, without bothering to explain the statement. "Juan Trippe is a good friend of mine, but if he thinks I'm going to let him have the West Indies all to himself he's very much mistaken. I'm going to make that the playground of the world. I'm going to make it possible for you to take your wife"—he paused to wave a finger at Sam—"or your girl, down there for five dollars a day."

He switched subjects abruptly.

"Do you have any idea how many airplanes I've given those Russians?" He didn't answer the question; a new thought had come to mind, about the French possessions in North America, a pair of small islands off the Newfoundland Grand Banks.

"If the French think they're going to keep Saint Pierre and Miquelon after the war they're very much mistaken."

Roosevelt paused briefly, then found another topic presumably of interest to an airline man. There had existed for some time the possibility that the Japanese might be able to take Alaska and the Aleutians. "So," the President said, "I'm sending Admiral Byrd on an expedition to find a new route across the Pacific."

The monologue ended and Sam concluded that the interview was over. Mumbling thanks, he departed. As he closed the outer door Sam noted by his watch that the interview had lasted 35 minutes; he wondered if he had stayed overlong and whether General Watson was muttering "Damned airlines."

Sam returned to the Carlton suite, where the other members of the committee were waiting to hear the outcome of the White House meeting. Before he could speak to them he was called to the telephone. The caller was Admiral Richard E. Byrd, the famous aviator and explorer, who had flown over the North Pole in the twenties and later led five expeditions to the Antarctic.

'I've been advised that the President informed you of my Pacific expedition," said the Admiral, "and that you promised him you would send a senior officer of your airline along with me. I would certainly appreciate that assistance."

Sam was taken aback. Although he was not quite sure what he had blurted to Roosevelt about the policy statement, he was fairly certain of what he had not said. But—the President was the President.

"I have no recollection of that, Admiral," Sam replied, "but far be it from me to dispute the President of the United States. I'll take care of it." Later, he dispatched Milton Anderson, thinking that the Pacific survey would only take two or three weeks; it took three months.

Sam turned to his committee, dejectedly. He felt he had let them down, because in his boyish awe of the President he had failed to punch home forcibly the arguments in support of their policy statement.

"I don't know why you made me chairman," he said, gloomily. "I fell down badly on this assignment. Come to think of it, I was a failure from the start; I even had trouble getting you out of the Pentagon."

But, Sam found a few weeks later, he had not muffed the assignment after all. Certainly, he had not been as eloquent with the President as he had planned to be, but whatever he had said, the presentation of the policy statement had borne fruit. On October 1, President Roosevelt called a press conference and issued his own statement on postwar airline policy, affirming in many respects the principles set forth by Solomon's committee.

He did not want to put the government into the postwar air passenger and freight business, the President announced; he advocated private ownership and operation of the airlines. Additionally, he stated, he had discussed matters with Prime Minister Winston Churchill and they had informally agreed on a "free air" policy, under which the world's airspace would be open to all nations and the airports built during the war available to every nation's airlines. Each nation would control all aviation within its borders, but reciprocal landing rights could be arranged by negotiation. The President did not specifically address himself to the question of monopoly or open competition.

The 16 airline signatories to the original policy statement regarded Roosevelt's endorsement as a major victory, but it was by no means the end of the battle for postwar status. Whatever policy emerged, it would have to be formalized by the Congress, either as a new law or an amendment to the existing Civil Aeronautics Act. And there were indications that a long struggle loomed ahead.

Pan American said little publicly, but no one doubted that the powerful airline would put up a strong fight for its chosen instrument concept. United's Patterson asserted emphatically that individual domestic airlines should be barred from international transocean service and he advocated either one or more chosen instruments or a joint pooling arrangement. On Capitol Hill, Chairman Josiah Bailey of the Senate Commerce Committee stated flatly: "One strong airline that could cope with the competition of foreign lines is the only sensible plan for postwar U.S. international air transportation." Others within the Congress also backed the chosen instrument approach.

Thus, the Airlines Committee for U.S. Air Policy entered a new phase of its operation. Having put its recommendations on record, it now turned to a public relations effort, to bring home to the nation's opinion leaders its views on open competition for overseas routes. To

Sam Solomon and the other members of the committee fell a new workload, traveling around the country addressing civic groups and speaking individually to Congressmen, state and local government officials, labor leaders, columnists, publishers and any others whose support might prove advantageous. It would have been an impossible task for Sam had not the Airlines War Training Institute suspended operations at about that time, but starting in November, 1943, he was back on his familiar two-job routine.

In April, 1944, Sam was in Las Vegas, Nevada, where he was to make one of his frequent speeches in opposition to the chosen instrument concept. There he encountered fellow committee member Jack Frye, president of TWA, and the noted aviator-industrialist-motion picture producer-billionaire Howard Hughes, who was controlling stockholder of TWA. Sam had met Hughes once before, in 1938, when Hughes had landed at Washington-Hoover Airport after a record flight in which he had circled the globe in less than four days.

Following the custom of the day, whereby airlines took delivery of California-built aircraft in Nevada to escape the California sales tax, Hughes and Frye were in Las Vegas to accept the first model of a new type of airliner, the Lockheed Constellation. As soon as the formalities of delivery were concluded, they were to take the four-engine "Connie" back to Burbank, California, from whence they would run a record-setting transcontinental flight to Washington the following day. Bigger and faster than any previous transport, the Connie should have no trouble breaking the existing record, which, incidentally, was held by Howard Hughes.

Sam was invited to go along. There would be a lot of publicity attendant upon the record run, Frye pointed out, and some of it might rub off on the airlines policy committee if Sam were aboard. Sam assented readily, but said he could not return to Burbank in the Connie because he still had to deliver his scheduled speech. He would join them there in time for the flight.

After the speech, Sam boarded an airliner and flew to Burbank, arriving long after midnight. In the dark, the Constellation, already undergoing its pre-flight warm-up and checkout, looked even larger than it was. Sam joined Hughes and Frye, waiting on the ramp. Hughes was casually garbed in sports clothes and tennis sneakers, the rest of his wardrobe for the trip draped over his arm.

"Howard," Frye was saying, "why don't you let me buy you a suitcase?"

Hughes said nothing. He rarely said anything, Sam noted. In fact, reflecting on it later, he could not recall any conversation with Hughes all the way across the country.

The pre-flight completed, the group boarded the airplane. Howard

Hughes took the pilot's seat, Frye the co-pilot's. With them in the cockpit were a navigator, a flight engineer and a radio operator. In the spacious pressurized cabin, built to seat 64, were a dozen passengers representing TWA, Lockheed and the Army Air Forces, which was buying a military version of the Constellation. Sam was the only one aboard who had no official connection with the flight.

Shortly before four a.m. on April 17, Hughes lifted the Connie off the Burbank runway and headed east. Flying at altitudes from 15,000 to 20,000 feet, a new realm for passenger flight, the triple-tailed Connie breezed across the continent at an average speed of 355 miles per hour. Six hours and 58 minutes after take-off, Hughes set the airplane down at Washington National Airport, trimming a half hour off the previous record.

Alerted by press notices, a large crowd had gathered to welcome the new sky-giant, among them Alma Solomon; Sam had had no time to call home, but a committee aide had relayed a terse message to "meet the Constellation." Newsmen flocked around Hughes, Frye and the passengers. The Washington papers were particularly interested in the presence on board of the local man who was also chairman of the airlines policy committee, and Sam had trouble convincing them that he had no official status. To one insistent reporter who asked what Sam had contributed to the flight, he replied:

"I contributed three dollars and fifty cents to the poker game." He added that it was a good thing the plane had set a record or he would have lost his shirt.

Sam flew back across the country to Seattle, to resume the talking trip he had interrupted to make the record flight. There he met Dave Beck, president of the powerful Teamsters' Union, whose support for the committee's views Sam very much wanted. Beck invited Sam to a private discussion in his office.

"Sam," Beck asked, by way of opening the conversation, "do you think I look like a labor leader or a bank president or a university trustee?"

"Bank president, maybe," Sam replied, "I don't know about labor leader. I never met one before."

They got along well. Beck listened with interest to Sam's recital of the policy committee's views. At the conclusion he summoned the editor of the Teamsters' house organ and ordered him to write an article endorsing the committee's policy. Sam left with assurance of further aid from Beck and, in fact, the labor leader did use his considerable influence later to gain support for open competition.

As chairman of the policy committee, Sam found himself in a personal conflict. More than a decade earlier, when he had embarked on the Boston-Maine Airways operation, he had made the acquaintance of Owen Brewster, then governor of Maine, and a strong friendship had grown over the years. Now Brewster, as a U.S. Senator, had become the most outspoken supporter of Pan American's chosen instrument concept. Sam wanted to preserve the friendship, but his airline colleagues were bitterly denouncing Brewster as a tool of Pan Am's Juan Trippe. Sam asked for a meeting and he was invited to breakfast in the Senator's Mayflower Hotel suite in Washington.

"Governor," Sam began—he always called Brewster governor—"I want to talk to you about your role in the airline dispute. The airlines are very much disappointed in you. They know you as a man with a broad knowledge of aviation and they had hoped you would be more of a factor in bringing about a sound postwar policy. Frankly, most of them believe you're in the pay of Pan American."

Brewster was disconcerted.

"I'm not," he replied. "But what do we do about it?"

"I think the question, governor, is what are *you* going to do about it." Sam left with the feeling that he might have made an impression on Brewster, but if he did it was short-lived. Brewster continued to support the chosen instrument, but despite their differences, the two remained friends.

In June, 1944, the Airlines Committee for U.S. Air Policy marked its first anniversary and Sam decided it was time for him to relinquish the chairmanship. If the committee was to retain its vigor, he told his fellow policymakers, it needed a transfusion of new blood. But, he added, he would like the right of final approval of the man they selected to succeed him.

The airlines picked Alec Royce, member of a New York law firm. Since Sam and Royce had never met, the lawyer flew to Washington for a get-acquainted meeting. In one session, Sam decided that Royce was the man for the job and he endorsed the nomination. Sam remained a member of the committee with the designation of treasurer.

Although he turned over the reins to Royce, Sam remained almost as active as he had been during his term as chairman. He had become widely known as the foremost opponent of the chosen instrument and champion of open airline competition, and he was in constant demand as a speaker. In addition, he arranged personal meetings with many of the nation's top-level opinion leaders.

The Airlines Committee for U.S. Air Policy continued to carry the battle against monopoly throughout the war years and into the postwar era. It never formally disbanded, it just faded away as the need for its efforts diminished. It was, from the standpoint of most of the airlines, a completely successful operation. The chosen instrument idea never got beyond the proposal stage. As it eventually emerged, the policy of the United States with regard to overseas commercial flight developed along the lines originally suggested in the committee's statement. Thus, the committee set a pattern which was to influence international air traffic from that day forward. And most would agree that the lion's share of the credit should properly go to the spearhead and guiding force of the airlines policy committee, Samuel J. Solomon.

CHAPTER X
Farewell to Northeast Airlines

By early 1943, Northeast Airlines' military operations in Canada and across the North Atlantic had become a matter of routine. Not that the flying could be called routine; it was anything but that, still largely a pioneering effort despite a year's experience. But the organizational job had been completed; Northeast's Military Division had been established, the requisite number of airplanes had been acquired from the Army Air Forces, route stations had been set up and the *modus operandi* had been refined.

The Military Division was functioning as smoothly as it ever could, considering the uncertainties of far north operations with twin-engine airplanes and the unpredictable nature of military requirements. From here on out, Northeast's operations staff could handle the military assignment; although Sam Solomon would continue to direct the overall program, he was now free to devote more of his time to the airline's commercial side.

There was, of course, nothing that could be done immediately to bolster the civilian portion of Northeast's operations. Passenger traffic, restricted to essential travel, was at low ebb and the airline's two civil DC-3's were more than adequate for the volume. But Sam, as always, was looking far ahead. The war would end sometime, and when it did he was certain that there would be an explosive growth of airline travel. The time to prepare for it was not at war's end, in the hectic helter-skelter of readjustment, but now.

If Northeast was to grow with air travel in general, the first requirement was a broadened route system. Northeast had started life as a local airline, operating entirely within northern New England. Commercially, it had expanded little beyond the initial route structure; the authorized system of less than 1,000 route miles would not be adequate for the type of growth that Sam envisioned.

Passengers from the north—from Bangor or Portland, from Burlington, Montpelier or Barre, for example—could fly Northeast to Boston. But frequently Boston was not the final destination; they had to take the train or another airline to complete the journey. This was not good airline service, in Solomon's estimation, and neither was it conducive to profitable operations. Sam wanted, first of all, to be able to provide through service to New York, from whence a passenger could make connections to anywhere. As a first step, he urged the Civil Aeronautics Board to get off dead center and start hearings on Northeast's application for a Boston-New York extension, a request that had been pending for almost five years.

Solomon, however, did not regard New York as the end-all, as did some of his fellow board members. He began to think in broader terms—a route westward from New York to Chicago and southward to Philadelphia, Washington and the deep South. And, looking in the other direction, Sam revived an old dream; the North Atlantic route to Europe, which he had first proposed in 1937.

At that time, Sam had been thinking solely in terms of flying to Scotland, Ireland and England. Now that his company had had a year's experience flying the North Atlantic, he revised his thinking. A study of operating costs, from data obtained on Northeast's military runs, convinced him that the route he had earlier envisioned would not—initially, at least—generate enough traffic to be self-supporting. Profitable service to Europe demanded a greater number of destinations and boarding points. Accordingly, Sam worked with Milton Anderson to draw up an overseas route system that could be flown at a profit in the postwar era by the large, four-engine transports already being built for war service.

On March 26, 1943, Northeast Airlines filed with the Civil Aeronautics Board an application that impacted on the aviation community like a bombshell. The application, the first of its kind ever filed by a domestic airline, sought authority to fly several routes across the Atlantic. One route would go via Newfoundland, Iceland, the Faroe Islands, Oslo, Stockholm and Leningrad to Moscow, with supplementary segments to Copenhagen and Prague. Another route would take Northeast directly over the North Atlantic to Glasgow and London, with additional service to Paris and Amsterdam. An alternate route would cross the Mid-Atlantic to the Azores, thence to London or Paris.

Announcement of the application was widely covered in the daily newspapers and the aviation trade press. To the man in the street, it was a fantastic proposal. The average person was aware that airplanes were flying the ocean, but only dimly, because wartime security cloaked the details. The idea of passenger travel to England in only 14 hours flying time, or to Moscow in 18, sounded like a page from Jules Verne.

Sam Solomon knew exactly what he was doing. He was aware that many would regard the application as a wild scheme. He was aware, too, that the Civil Aeronautics Board would not likely take action during wartime and that the CAB would consider the proposed European route system a very large bite for a small airline. But there was a lot of thought behind the action.

At the time, the airlines policy committee had not yet been formed but Sam was already making speeches advocating free and open airline competition after the war. In filing the application, Sam was telling the world that Northeast had accumulated a wealth of experience in military transocean flying and that the airline fully expected to continue that type of service in the postwar era. In addition, he was serving notice of Northeast's conviction that privately-owned airlines should fly the postwar international airlanes, an advance counterploy against the then-rumored possibility that U.S. international operations would be handled by a government airline.

Among airline people, the proposal was greeted by some with open ridicule; others, the more thoughtful of the aviation community, saw the method behind Solomon's apparent madness. One such was Wayne W. Parrish, the foremost aviation writer of the day, who wrote in American Aviation magazine:

"Astute Sam Solomon caused plenty of eyebrow-raising and even some chuckling when he filed an application for Northeast Airlines, of which he is president, to fly scheduled service to Moscow and a score of European cities and capitals. More power to him. Sam Solomon knows that if private industry sits quietly by, biding its time and being shy about postwar plans, that government-owned airline operation is just around the corner. Outcries are few when government pioneers where private enterprise has never evinced any interest, but there will be outcries if government attempts to take away something that private enterprise wants and is capable of performing. If private initiative is to remain in its rightful place, it had better not lag behind too long, or too long may turn out to be too late."

Business Week magazine also offered a comment:

"Airline operators laughed when Northeast Airlines, New England's local, filed an application with the Civil Aeronautics Board for a regular 5,000-mile route between Boston and Moscow—but on second thought they wished that they had also filed their claims . . . The other airlines hate to drop their dignity and holler 'me too,' but they are worried." In fact, the other airlines *did* "holler me too;" they followed where Solomon had led, some of the laughers included, and there was a flurry of applications for overseas routes.

Just three weeks after the European route filing, Solomon and Northeast Airlines gave the Civil Aeronautics Board some additional food for thought with another "first of its kind" application, this time for helicopter service. This idea had its inception earlier in the year, when Sam Solomom attended a demonstration of a Sikorsky helicopter at Bridgeport, Connecticut.

It seems hard to believe today that the familiar helicopter, work horse of a hundred uses in wide service throughout the world, was no more than an experimental curio in 1943. Its inventor, Russian-born Igor Sikorsky, had been researching for several years what he called a "direct lift aircraft"—the helicopter. In 1940 he had made the first flight and by 1941 he had developed a practical machine capable of remaining aloft for an hour. The following year he received his first military contract for a "rotary wing machine" and in 1942-43 he was flying a refined version of his original civil helicopter, the VS-300, and demonstrating it to aviation people. At that time, few people had ever seen a helicopter and, because it was being developed under military contract, only the scantiest information had reached the press.

At the Bridgeport demonstration, the Sikorsky machine created quite a stir. The small craft was little more than an open frame topped by a large rotor. At the end of the fuselage—what would have been the tail of an airplane—was a small auxiliary rotor, used to counteract the torque of the main lifting rotor. The cockpit was simply a seat wedged into the framework with a set of controls at the operator's front and side. A pair of rubber floats served as landing gear.

Igor Sikorsky personally took the controls and ran the craft through a series of maneuvers, straight up and down, from side to side, and hovering in still flight. It was a fascinating performance and no one was more excited by it than Sam Solomon.

"Listen," he said to Sikorsky after the demonstration, "you get this machine perfected so it will land on my front lawn and I'll buy one for my wife."

Sam realized, of course, that it would be a very long time before there would be any front-lawn flying. But the demonstration had made a tremendous impression on him and it kept running through his mind for weeks thereafter. Sam was well aware that the helicopter had barely begun to toddle and that years of painstaking development lay ahead before the machine could become a practicable commercial vehicle. He was equally aware, however, that airplane development in general had moved at an incredible pace in the 40 years since the first powered flights, that the pace was accelerating under the impetus of wartime necessity, and that the helicopter would probably spring to maturity more rapidly than most people thought it would.

Commercial helicopter operations need not await the day when it would be feasible to carry passengers on a paying basis, Sam Solomon reasoned. Even a small "whirly-bird," such as the craft Sikorsky had demonstrated, could break into service as a mail carrier, hippity-hopping to hundreds of small communities not regularly served by airlines. Mail service could provide the operating experience which would serve as a springboard to full development of the rotary-wing machine as a passenger carrier.

So, once again displaying the vision which few of his contemporaries could match, Sam Solomon filed the first application for commercial service on April 8, 1943. Northeast's proposal to the Civil Aeronautics Board asked authority to fly, in the postwar period, helicopter service to more than 400 stations in the six New England states and New York. The application envisioned operations between cities and towns, airports and post offices, airports and railroad stations, and post offices and railroad stations. It focused on mail service but included a provision for a passenger-carrying aerial taxi service at such time as development of the rotary-wing vehicle would permit.

The application created as broad an interest as had the European route filing. The CAB, of course, did not act upon it during the war years. In fact, many postwar years were to elapse before the Board got around to considering commercial helicopter service and when it did Northeast Airlines was not among the successful bidders. Nonetheless, the application was regarded as a personal triumph for Sam Solomon. He had focused attention upon a brand new area of aviation development with broad potential and he inspired thought and planning on the part of other people as regards the commercial utility of the helicopter. In the postwar years, helicopter advancement did, in fact, progress along the lines Sam had envisioned; the whirly-bird started commercial life as an experimental mail carrier, moved into unscheduled passenger-taxi operations and eventually became a short-haul transport for scheduled passenger service. Sam's own enthusiasm for the helicopter did not end with the Northeast application; it was to continue throughout his career.

Although Sam's Northeast work during this period centered on commercial operations planning, he never abandoned his interest and personal contact with the company's Military Division. In spite of the rigorous travel schedule demanded by his multiple jobs, he found time for frequent visits to the Military Division's base at Presque Isle to assure himself that the war-support effort was functioning smoothly.

On one of his trips to Presque Isle, Sam encountered a minor crisis. Northeast was operating an all-night truck service between the air base and a downtown hotel, shuttling flight crews and line personnel. On this occasion, the night truck driver had not reported for duty; there was no replacement available and none of the busy flight line people could be spared.

So Sam Solomon, president of the company, rolled up his sleeves and became a truck driver. Throughout a long night he drove back and forth from the airport to the hotel. In the morning he climbed stiffly from the cab of the truck, so tired it took all his remaining energy to register in the hotel and move into the room assigned him. The room had not been made up. The bed was thoroughly soaked from a wet bath towel the previous occupant had tossed on it. It didn't seem to make any difference; Sam fell on the bed and slept soundly.

Sam also kept in touch with activities at the company-operated training school in Burlington, Vermont; he had a dual interest, as Northeast's president and also as president of the Airlines War Training Institute. He often told the story of an amusing conversation in a typically Vermontese vein that took place on one of his visits.

Since moving into Burlington a year earlier, the school had continued to expand. Northeast was now building a new hangar at Burlington Airport and there was also a need for additional classroom space. The Burlington School Board had an unused facility and Milton Anderson, who had primary responsibility for the training program, was going to Burlington to negotiate purchase of the building. Sam, who had other business in Burlington, went along.

Anderson sat with officials of the school board, but Sam took no part in the initial discussion. After meeting the board members, Sam departed for another engagement, to talk with the mayor and city officials about improving Northeast's service to Burlington. He returned some time later to find that negotiations with the school board had not progressed an iota.

"What's the problem?" Sam asked.

"Well, Mr. Solomon," said the chairman of the school board in a slow, Vermont drawl, "We asked for $10,000, although we really didn't expect to get that much. And Captain Anderson here, he offered $5,000, although I'm sure he didn't expect us to settle for that. And that's where we stand."

In typical Solomon let's-get-it-done-right-now fashion, Sam suggested:

"Well, why don't we split the difference? How about $7,500?"

The school board head seemed a trifle downcast at this abrupt solution.

"I guess that would be all right, Mr. Solomon," he drawled, "But we surely would like to bargain a little more."

In September, 1943, the Civil Aeronautics Board was finally ready to consider Northeast's application of five years' standing for a Boston-New York route. But, as hearings opened in Washington, a new problem reared its head. Ever since the passage of the Civil Aeronautics Act in 1938, there had been a question, never resolved, as to whether railroad interests should be permitted to control an airline. With the dusting off of Northeast's New York application, the question was revived.

The three railroad participants in Northeast Airlines collectively owned some 40 percent of the stock, by far the largest single block. This, the Board implied, amounted to railroad control, despite Sam Solomon's testimony that he and not the railroads ran the airline. The Board never stated flatly that the New York application would be disapproved by virtue of railroad control, but there were indications that his and other planned expansions would be stymied if the matter was not resolved.

In a magnanimous gesture, the executives of the participating railroads decided to reduce their holdings in the interest of the airline's future. While the hearings were under way, they negotiated the sale of 100,000 shares of stock, reducing their combined interest to something less than 10 percent. Fifty thousand shares were acquired by Atlas Corporation, a holding company directed by financier Floyd Odlum. This, together with stock previously held by Atlas, made the holding company the largest single stockholder in Northeast Airlines.

The change of control had no immediate effect on Northeast's operations. The board elected two new directors to represent Atlas Corporation's interest. One of them was Mrs. Odlum, the internationally-famous aviatrix, Jacqueline Cochrane; the other was Radu Irimescu, a one-time commissioner of aviation in Roumania. Sam Solomon enjoyed good relations with Odlum, "Jackie" Cochrane Odlum and Irimescu and they supported him in his direction of the company.

The Board, satisfied on the issue of railroad control, finally granted Northeast the right to expand to New York early in January, 1944. To Sam Solomon, it was a gratifying verdict, the attainment of a long-standing objective. With that chapter closed, Sam decided the time had come for him to effect a change in his personal career pattern.

For several months, he had been giving a lot of thought to his status with Northeast. A major influence was the fact that he was physically and mentally tired. For almost 11 years, except for a brief period following closure of Washington-Hoover Airport, Sam had been living the multiple-occupation existence with its wearying travel and mental gear-shifting. For five months in 1943, he had had not the usual two but three major jobs. The shutdown of the Airlines War Training Institute had partially reduced his workload, but the difference was hardly noticeable, so demanding were the two remaining jobs. Now 44, Sam wanted to go home to Silver Spring, to spend some time with his family, to sit around his pool and chat with friends, to pass glorious weeks at a time without having to dash for an airplane.

There was another influence. For some time his relationships with Paul Collins, still serving as Northeast's board chairman, and with Gene Vidal, still a stockholder, had been deteriorating. Collins and Vidal, though by no means unpatriotic, had never shared Sam's fervor for support of the military transport effort; they felt that Sam had committed too great a portion of the corporate energies to war service and that commercial development was being stifled as a result.

Perhaps, too, there was some resentment. Sam Solomon, although he had never actively sought prominence, had become a nationally-known, even internationally-known figure in the aviation world while they had remained in obscurity. At any rate, the easy camaraderie among the partners that had characterized the fledgling years of the airline no longer existed.

Sam's interest in Northeast Airlines had not waned; far from it. He was proud of the airline's record, proud of his role in giving it life and still very much concerned with its future development. Had the weariness occasioned by his multiple jobs been the only factor, no doubt he could have made some adjustment. But the added influence of dissension within the company convinced him that it would be better for all concerned, the airline included, if he stepped down from the presidency. Reluctant to sever completely his ties with Northeast, he felt that perhaps he could continue to serve in an advisory capacity. Thus shorn of the day-to-day workload, he would be free to devote his primary energies to the chairmanship of the airlines policy committee.

Late in 1943, while the Boston-New York case was still being heard in endless argument and counter-argument, Sam went to Floyd Odlum and aired his views with respect to his status with Northeast, concluding that he would probably resign the presidency. Odlum and the Roumanian Irimescu sought to dissuade him.

"We'll give you complete support," they told him, "We'll back any policy you advocate or any program you want to follow."

Sam said only that he would remain on the job until the Civil Aeronautics Board came up with a decision on expansion to New York.

That matter successfully concluded, Sam reached a final decision. At a board meeting on January 15, 1944, he tendered his resignation as president. The board reluctantly accepted, elected Paul Collins president and asked Sam to take over the board chairmanship vacated by Collins. He agreed.

Shortly after his stepdown from the presidency, Sam returned to his Washington policy committee office. His secretary informed him that he had had a number of calls from one Joe Bernhard, vice president of Warner Brothers. Sam couldn't imagine what a movie mogul wanted from him, but he returned the call and agreed to meet with Bernhard.

Bernhard, it turned out, wanted to buy control of Northeast Airlines from Floyd Odlum. But, Odlum had told him, the airline would not be worth buying unless Sam Solomon could be persuaded to return. Sam was noncommittal.

"Tell me," Bernhard asked, "how many airplanes does Northeast own?"

"Two," Sam replied.

"Two?" Bernhard seemed startled. "Odlum wants two million. A million an airplane, that's a lot of money." He shrugged it off. "What the hell, in Hollywood sometimes we buy a book for half a million, put it on the shelf and forget it."

So, how about it, Bernhard asked. If he, Bernhard, could acquire control of Northeast, would Sam agree to resume active management?

Hesitantly, Sam said that he would consider the proposal. A couple of weeks had elapsed since he had resigned as president of Northeast and in that time he had found that the rest he had sought was not as attractive as he had thought it would be; "I rest fast," he told friends. He wrestled with himself over Bernhard's offer but in the end decision became unnecessary; Bernhard and Odlum never reached a meeting of the minds and the control purchase fell through.

So, for the next 15 months, Sam devoted the major portion of his time to his duties with the airlines policy committee. He remained active with Northeast, however. He continued to serve as company spokesman, the other officers and board members deferring to his acknowledged stature in the aviation community. As chairman of the board, he focused his attention on broad policy matters and plans for future development. In the latter regard, he brought to the board a sweeping proposal for a brand new type of service.

At that time, all airlines offered one-class service; the lower-fare coach or economy class seating was not in existence. Someone had thought of it, though—Sam Solomon. Why not, Sam argued, borrow a page from the railroads' book and offer a low-cost "day coach" service, thereby enormously broadening the market of people who could afford to travel by air? He made a two-point suggestion to the Northeast board: that the airline should seek a major expansion of its route structure by applying to the Civil Aeronautics Board for additional routes to Philadelphia, Washington and the deep South; and, assuming the routes were granted, that Northeast should offer lower-fare coach service over its entire system.

The Northeast board was cool to the proposal. Having acquired the route extension to New York, the company's directors were content to let it go at that; Sam's proposed route additions seemed too grandiose a plan. Lacking Sam's vision, they could not see the tremendous potential of broadening the market base by the introduction of low-fare service; it seemed to them that Sam's concept was nothing more than a fare reduction and they were having trouble making ends meet at regular fares. The idea was rejected.

Sam was dismayed, but not particularly surprised, at his colleagues' myopia. He knew as surely as if he could look into the future that the day coach concept would revolutionize air travel. Sam served notice on his fellow directors: he intended to push for low-fare service, if not with Northeast, then independently. He informed them that, in the not-too-distant future, he planned to form a new airline based on the coach idea.

Sam Solomon had another opportunity to retake direction of the airline, or, more properly, a greatly expanded airline of which Northeast would be a part. It came in a luncheon meeting with Robert Lehman of Lehman Brothers and Benjamin F. Pepper, who headed Pennroad Corporation. After Atlas Corporation, Lehman Brothers and Pennroad held the largest blocks of stock in Northeast Airlines, acquired in the 1943 redistribution when the railroads had reduced their holdings.

"I bet on people more than balance sheets," Bobby Lehman told Sam, "and I bought into Northeast because of you." To which Pepper added, "Likewise."

Lehman and Pepper had an interesting proposal for Sam's consideration. In addition to his interest in Northeast, Lehman was also banker for National Airlines, a Miami-based company operating along the East Coast from Florida to New York. He and Pepper thought they could put together a deal involving a merger of Northeast and National, which would produce a strong single airline with authorized routes stretching from Canada to the southern tip of the United States. If they could swing the deal, they wanted Sam Solomon as chief executive. How did Sam feel about it?

Sam thought it over. The principal obstacle, as he saw it, was National's tough, hard-headed president Ted Baker. Sam knew Baker and respected him as a businessman, but he saw no way in which he and Baker could work as a team.

It would be unfair to Baker, Sam Told Lehman, and bad for the merged company, if Sam moved in over Baker.

"Baker should logically get first offer of the top job," he said, "because National is the larger airline." And as for the possibility of Sam's taking second place in the proposed airline, that was out of the question. 'I couldn't work under Ted Baker for 10 minutes." So Sam declined any participation in the merger idea, which died in concept.

In Boston on Northeast business, Sam had lunch with John Sargent of Roosevelt and Sargent, who represented the airline's insurance underwriters. Sargent, a partner of the President's son Jimmy Roosevelt and also close to Mrs. Eleanor Roosevelt, confided to Sam that the President was extremely ill and that his death could come at any time. It was a shocking revelation; no hint of Franklin Roosevelt's condition had reached the public ear.

The next day, back in Washington, Sam visited with his long-time friend, Senator Owen Brewster. Pledging Brewster to secrecy, Sam related what Sargent had told him.

"What kind of a President will Harry Truman make?" Sam asked. Brewster knew Truman well, having served with him on the Truman committee investigating war contracts.

"I think he'll make a great President," the Senator replied. Sam was impressed, even amazed, at this remark from one of the most ardent of all Republicans about the capabilities of a Democrat. He never forgot it and he later concurred in Brewster's opinion, as did most of America and the world.

It was shortly thereafter, in mid-April of 1945, that Sam went to Havana, Cuba, to represent Northeast at a conference. Executives of most of the nation's airlines, along with officials of a number of foreign carriers, were gathering to initiate formation of an International Air Transport Association, a coordinating body which would work toward greater air safety, operational efficiency and a stable fare structure.

While Sam was in Havana, word was flashed around the world that Franklin Delano Roosevelt had died. And on the same day Sam received another item of news: Northeast Airlines, in his absence, had announced plans to file for route extensions to the southern United States.

Sam was shocked and angered. Only a short time earlier, the Northeast board had rejected his southern service idea as too ambitious. There seemed only one explanation for the sudden about-face: Northeast's directors were making a pre-emptive move, attempting to erect a roadblock to his own plans for a new airline which would serve the Eastern Seaboard on a low-fare basis.

Sam flew back to Boston and immediately tendered his resignation as chairman of the board. In addition, he began to divest himself of his considerable stock holdings. For one thing, he was now firmly resolved to go ahead with the formation of the new airline and he would need personal capital.

It was a severe wrench to cut all ties with the airline he had served for 12 years, but Northeast had left him no alternative. He would have soon severed his Northeast connection anyway, because the coach service concept had been occupying more and more of his thinking and, with the end of World War II imminent, it was time to move out in this new direction.

CHAPTER XI

Solomon's Atlantic Airlines

Once Sam Solomon had made the final decision to get out of Northeast Airlines and proceed with organization of the new company, things moved with Solomonlike swiftness. Within two months after he left Northeast, Sam had a company, a bank account, an office and a staff, and he was putting the finishing touches to the detailed application he would present to the Civil Aeronautics Board.

The company Sam named Atlantic Airlines, Inc. From the money obtained through sale of some of his Northeast stock, Sam put up the first $70,000. A number of Sam's former associates joined with him in the venture: Edward S. French, president of the Boston and Maine Railroad; Laurence Whittemore, the visionary railroader who had sparked air service in New England; Benjamin F. Pepper of Pennroad Corporation; and Joe Bernhard, the Warner Brothers executive who had once sought control of Northeast. There were nearly a score of others, and in no case did Sam have to solicit their interest; the word was out that Solomon had a new project and investors came in over the transom. Atlantic Airlines started life with a capitalization of $225,000.

This amount would cover staff salaries and day-to-day expenses during the predictably lengthy period covering the filing of an application, hearings before the CAB, and post-hearing deliberations by the Board. When and if the application was approved, considerably greater funding would be required. Sam estimated it would take between $4 and $5 million to buy airplanes, hire additional people, set up route stations and begin operations. To handle that financing, when it was needed, Sam lined up the services of an underwriting group headed by J. A. W. Iglehart, a banker with W. E. Hutton & Company, one of the foremost stock exchange houses.

Atlantic Airlines had a ready-made headquarters—the suite in the Carlton Hotel which Sam had rented two years earlier for the use of the airlines policy committee. The committee had never formally disbanded, but its work was largely completed and it had no further need of an office. Sam was happy to take over the suite, thereby eliminating some of the confusion that usually attends the start of a new venture in an unfamiliar atmosphere.

The necessity of breaking in a new secretary/right-hand aide was obviated when Ruth Basius elected to join Atlantic; Ruth had been with Sam at Northeast, at the Airlines War Training Institute and again with the airlines policy committee. Another familiar face was Ben Cole, who had once directed Northeast's training school. Among the newcomers were Morrie Bernhard, son of Joe Bernhard and a transport-qualified pilot who had served in the Navy, and Vince Conroy, a former vice president of TWA and an airline traffic expert.

Sam Solomon's operational plan for Atlantic Airlines, though bold and revolutionary, was simple in essence. The idea was to fill more seats by making air transportation available to communities which had no air service and to people who felt they could not pay the higher costs of air travel as compared with surface movement. Atlantic would have more seats per airplane than competitive airlines and hopefully would have a higher load factor—the percentage of available seats filled on a given flight. Through this combination of economic factors, Sam felt he could almost halve existing airline fares and still operate profitably without air mail subsidy.

The major attraction of Atlantic Airlines would be the fact that a ticket entitled the passenger not simply to transportation between two airports, but from hometown departure point to a downtown area at final destination. Sam and his staff checked out this possibility with a number of bus operators in a number of cities and towns and found it entirely feasible.

A study of existing airline fares showed that, on the average, the passenger paid 4.85 cents per mile for the air portion of his journey alone. Getting to and from the airport was a heavy additional cost, because surface transport operators, aware that the usually-prosperous airline passenger was a good mark, were getting some stiff prices for the ground portion of a trip. Therefore, an overall trip, from start to destination, ran more than six cents a mile. Sam Solomon's Atlantic Airlines proposed to offer the total air-ground package at three and a half cents per mile, and in addition to the low-fare attraction there was a convenience bonus in bus service to and from outlying communities which had no air service.

The key to the plan was a sharp reduction in airline operating costs. Atlantic's studies showed that airlines were spending one-third of their fare revenues to operate a reservations control system, sell tickets, check in customers at the airport, check baggage, load and unload baggage, provide ramp service to and from the airplane, and to serve free meals aloft. Atlantic proposed to spend only one-fifth of its much lower fare on ground-handling of passengers, by eliminating "frills."

To begin with, Atlantic would offer no meal service; Sam felt it was not necessary on the short and medium haul routes he planned to fly and that the passengers he was seeking to attract—the average, not-wealthy middle class travelers—would prefer the monetary saving. Elimination of this "frill" would save the cost of the meal itself, its delivery to the airplane by a caterer and the flight attendants needed to serve it.

Aside from these cost reductions, however, there was another, more important factor: elimination of the bulky airplane galley would make it possible to install additional seats without compromising passenger comfort. For example, on the DC-3 which Sam was planning to fly initially, removal of the galley would increase capacity to 28 seats, compared with the 21-24 seats in the DC-3's being flown by other airlines. That meant four to seven additional fares when the plane was full, and it was likely to be full often at the fare levels Sam Solomon contemplated.

There were other planned economies. Atlantic would eschew the elaborate and cumbersome reservations and ticketing systems employed by other airlines. Instead, Atlantic would operate high-frequency schedules wherein a passenger could generally count on a seat without making a reservation. Tickets would be purchased either on the bus en route to the airport, or on the airplane from a "flight manager." Passengers would carry their own baggage to and from the airplane; the flight manager would help them stow it and check each passenger aboard. Thus, a single flight manager per airplane would replace the squads of ground personnel normally needed at each station on the route for reservations, ticketing, check-in and baggage handling.

Atlantic Airlines came up with another important innovative idea—integral stairs, or mechanically-operated boarding steps built into the airplane. David Morrow, an Atlantic engineer, designed a set of steps for the DC-3 and built a one-quarter scale working model for display to the CAB. The stairs naturally entailed a weight penalty, but it was not important in the short-range type of service Atlantic planned. Offsetting the additional weight were a number of advantages: with built-in steps, Atlantic would not have to buy expensive, wheeled loading ramps, several of which might be required at major stations; passengers could be loaded and off-loaded more rapidly, cutting down on ground time; and there would be a further personnel reduction, since there would be no need for people to wheel the boarding ramp into place.

Through the combination of all these devices, Atlantic hoped to realize a substantial reduction in operating costs, particularly salaries. It was estimated that, for the eight million passenger miles a year that Atlantic planned to fly, an airline operating under conventional practices would require 339 ground personnel. Atlantic would

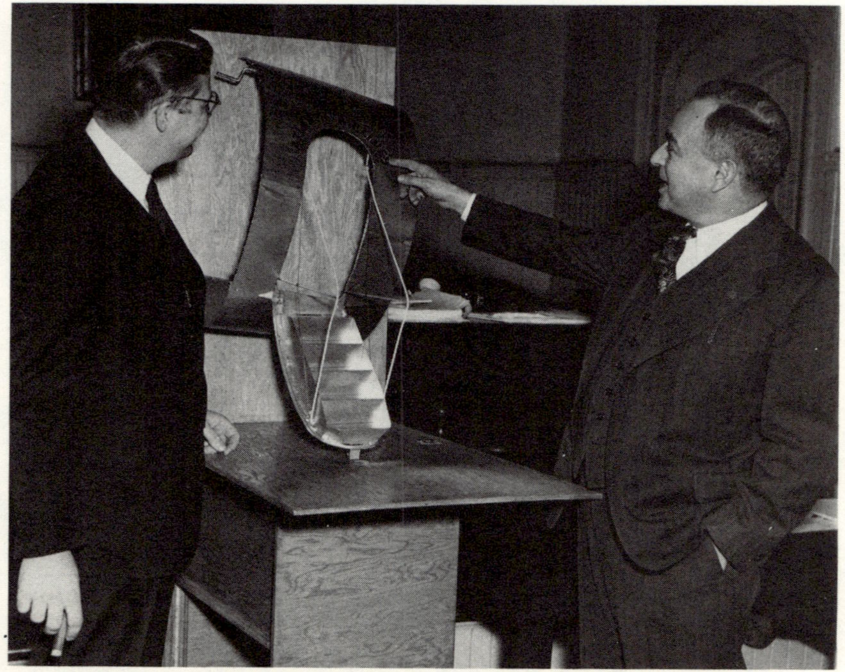

Sam Solomon (right) uses a scale model of Atlantic Airlines' integral stairs to explain to Civil Aeronautics Board Examiner Charles Frederick the details of the time-saving, mechanically-operated boarding steps designed to be built into a transport airplane. Atlantic was first to come up with the idea of integral stairs.

need only 86. The reduction in salaries and other terminal costs would be passed on to the passenger in the form of a lower price per ticket. That, in turn, coupled with the attraction of all-the-way convenience, would inevitably bring higher load factors and permit Atlantic to make a profit without subsidy.

Economics aside, the big thing in Sam Solomon's view was that the Atlantic formula would make air transportation available to millions of people who had never flown because of the high fare level. It was estimated that little more than a quarter of a million people, out of a U.S. population of 130,000,000, were making use of the domestic airlines; although statistics showed much larger numbers being boarded, they were the same people "flying over and over again until the seats of their pants got shiny," to quote Colonel Edgar S. Gorrell, president of the Air Transport Association.

Air travel, Sam insisted, should not be a privilege reserved for the wealthy or the expense-account business flyer. The U.S. airline system, he argued, had been developed through government subsidies and therefore it belonged to all the taxpayers. In the long run, Solomon knew, all airlines would benefit from a broadened market, but he didn't expect the entrenched air transport companies to acknowledge that aspect of his proposal; collectively, airline executives were not noted for foresight, and they would more likely be concerned with the immediate competitive threat.

On July 2, Sam Solomon, president of Atlantic Airlines, Inc., filed an application with the CAB requesting the right to provide air service linking New England with the deep South, such service to be offered "without luxuries and without frills and with an all-inclusive low fare that would include transportation to and from the airport."

Specifically, the application sought routes from Providence, Rhode Island (a substitute for Boston in order to stay away from Northeast Airlines' major cities) to New Orleans, Louisiana, running through such major cities as New York, Philadelphia, Baltimore, Washington, Richmond, Atlanta and Birmingham and including stops at 26 other points. Since bus connecting service would be available to smaller towns within 50 miles of each of the route stations, air travel would be opened up to literally hundreds of communities which at that time enjoyed no regular airline service.

"In my opinion," said Sam Solomon in an accompanying statement, "it is time that the airlines of the United States provide service at rates that compare with present air travel costs as day coach rates on a railroad compare with Pullman. This is what Atlantic Airlines proposes to do at the earliest possible date."

Announcement of the Atlantic Airlines plan excited wide interest. The press and the general public greeted the proposal warmly, but there was a distinct lack of enthusiasm among the airline industry. Airline people generally took the attitude that air transportation was a premium service, that people should expect to pay more for the speed and convenience that the airplane afforded.

One airline head—C. Bedell Monro, president of Pennsylvania-Central Airlines—ridiculed the idea of passengers carrying their own baggage onto and off of the airplane. He had tried it, he said, and he didn't like it. That effectively dismissed the concept as far as C. Bedell Monro was concerned. Actually, Monro's own airline—some time later when he was no longer president—introduced coach service with a do-it-yourself baggage-handling system and found that passengers were perfectly willing to carry their own luggage in return for a substantial fare reduction.

Airline executives also pointed out that they were already trimming their rates; only a few months earlier there had been a reduction in fares. This was true enough on the surface, but Sam Solomon brought up an influencing factor that the airlines had failed to mention. There was in effect a wartime excess profits tax. To avoid paying heavy additional taxes, the airlines had to keep their profits within certain bounds. So they simply lowered fares to escape the surtax. With the end of the war imminent, it appeared that the excess profits tax would soon be repealed. When that happened, Solomon forecast, some of the incentive to reduce fares would be removed, and it appeared quite possible that fares would go up instead of down. That, Sam felt, made his proposal doubly important.

Atlantic Airlines' application, of course, was only one of many to be considered. In the months preceding and following the end of World War II, practically all of the airlines had filed petitions for extensions of their authorized route structures, seeking to solidify their route systems for the peacetime travel boom that everyone was predicting. The Civil Aeronautics Board split the applications into a number of separate cases, each case covering a certain geographical area of the United States and each involving several petitioners. For each case the Board assigned an Examiner, a sort of interim judge who would hear and sift the evidence introduced by the various route-seekers and make recommendations to the five-man Board as to who should be assigned what route segments.

Thus, Atlantic Airlines' application was not considered as a whole; instead it became part of two separate cases and in each instance there were a number of other airlines competing for identical or overlapping route segments. Sam Solomon's petition for routes south of Washington to New Orleans was lumped with similar requests for service in the Southeast; the CAB procedure was designated the New Orleans Case. The rest of the Atlantic Airlines' proposal, for service north of Washington and west as far as Pittsburgh, was thrown into the Middle Atlantic Case.

Hearings before the Examiners, always long-drawn-out affairs as each of the competing companies stated its own views and presented arguments against its rivals, got under way in 1946. Atlantic Airlines was a particular target of the various spokesmen because it was not an operating entity; Solomon was requesting a new certificate for scheduled service and the airlines opposed admission of new companies to the nation's air transport system on the grounds that there were already enough carriers. The entrenched operators also argued that, if day-coach service were desirable—and none of them believed that it was—then they could provide it.

The fact remained, however, that no other airline was proposing low-fare service. Sam Solomon's application was unique, the first ever received by the Board for air coach operations at substantially reduced fares. Together with the fact that Sam Solomon was offering to operate without government subsidy, this gave rise to the hope that the Board might grant Atlantic a certificate as an experiment, to see what effect such a major service innovation would have on the traveling public.

About the time the Board hearings started, Sam Solomon was given an opportunity to head up another airline. Sam's old friends Jack Frye and Ben Pepper had bought control of TACA Airways, an international carrier operating from the United States to Central and South America. They asked Sam if he would consider taking over the top job in TACA.

Sam didn't have to think it over very long. He was entirely wrapped up in Atlantic Airlines and TACA did not lend itself to the two-job routine, even if Sam had been disposed to try that rugged mode again. He declined the offer. Frye and Pepper then asked him for alternative recommendations and he provided a couple of names. One of them was Major General Thomas O. Hardin (USAF, Retired), whom Sam had known as a pilot and a competent operations man since the Washington-Hoover Airport days. Frye and Pepper decided Hardin was their man.

"I must say this, though," Sam cautioned, "since you're accepting my recommendation. I have complete confidence in Hardin as a pilot and an operations man, but you've got to remember that all his executive service has been with the power of the U.S. Treasury and the Air Force behind him."

It was a prophetic caution. Hardin, stepping into an unfamiliar atmosphere, had nothing but trouble, particularly with the Latin governments involved in TACA's operation. The airline lost several million dollars, Hardin resigned and finally Frye and Pepper also pulled out of TACA.

As the Board cases progressed through 1946, Sam Solomon was essentially a one-job man, most of his time being taken by the CAB hearings and by planning for Atlantic's future operations. He did not lack for other interests, however. He was now a director of the YMCA and he was also active in the Aero Club of Maryland, the Aero Club of Washington and the U.S. Chamber of Commerce. And suddenly he found himself involved in a brand new field—automobile sales.

A few months after the end of World War II, Harry Harris, a long-time friend of Sam Solomon, had asked Sam's help. Harris wanted to start an auto sales agency, but he had not been successful in attempts to obtain a franchise. Did Sam, with his wide range of contacts, know anyone who could intercede?

Sam did, in fact, know someone. In his days with Northeast Airlines, Sam had met and become quite friendly with Harlan Pierpoint, a director of Nash Motor Corporation. Sam called Pierpoint and sought his assistance.

The call brought action. A Nash representative visited Sam in Washington and informed him apologetically that the company had no franchise vacancies in the Washington area.

"But," he added, "there is an opening in Norfolk which we could assign you."

"Wait a minute," said Sam. "It's not for me. I was simply trying to help a friend get a franchise."

"Oh, I'm afraid we can't do that," the Nash man replied. "My instructions are to assign the franchise only to Sam Solomon."

"Well," said Sam, who had no especial interest in auto sales but would not let a friend down if he could help it, "If that's the way it has to be, I'll take it."

So Sam became a one-third owner of a Nash dealership in Norfolk. He and Harry Harris organized Harris Motors, Inc., with Harris as president, Sam as vice president, and M. N. "Mike" Klein, a former Nash service representative, as secretary and general manager. They erected a large, modern sales and service center and opened for business in August, 1946.

It was early in 1947 that Sam read a news item which amazed and angered him. James Ray, a vice president of Southwest Airways, a "feeder" airline, had applied for a patent for self-containing loading stairs, built into the door of an airliner to facilitate passenger boarding and egress.

This, of course, was the same system that had been invented by David Morrow of Atlantic Airlines. A year earlier, Sam Solomon had displayed a model of the integral steps to the CAB, as part of his testimony in the Middle Atlantic Case. Sam had subsequently announced that Atlantic Airlines would not patent the invention, but would make it available to all airlines in the interests of American air transportation. James Ray had dropped by Atlantic's office at the Carlton Hotel and had requested permission to study the engineering drawings of the integral steps and take notes. Thinking that Ray intended only to introduce the innovation to Southwest Airways' operations, Sam had readily assented. Now Ray was seeking to patent an Atlantic Airlines' concept.

When the patent was later granted, Sam was doubly furious. For a while he entertained the idea of bringing legal action against Ray, but in the end he dropped it; he felt that the patent would not stand up if challenged, by virtue of the fact that Atlantic Airlines' prior display of the concept was on record. Additionally, the aviation trade journals had well covered Ray's patent filing and Sam's comments of protest and there was no doubt in the industry as to the real source of the integral steps idea, which was in later years to find wide acceptance among aircraft designers.

In the spring of 1947, the Board Examiners issued reports on the cases in which Atlantic Airlines was involved. There was bad news and good news. In the New Orleans Case, the Examiner rejected Atlantic's request for a Washington-New Orleans-intermediate cities route. But in the Middle Atlantic Case the Examiner recommended that Atlantic Airlines be granted a "certificate of public convenience and necessity" authorizing service over a roughly triangular route system bounded by Washington, New York and Pittsburgh, with 10 intermediate stops.

"This conclusion is reached," read the Examiner's report, "with the full realization that the allegation is made that service similar to that proposed by Atlantic could be provided by any carrier. Be that as it may, the fact is that proposals to provide a new type service standing in relationship to present airline service as bus and rail coach service stand in relationship to Pullman type service have not been forthcoming from the certificated carriers. Yet it appears that the Middle Atlantic Area is the section of the country where such a proposal, if put into experimental operation, would undergo the best tests for success or failure. If it is a success here, the large reservoir of new traffic generated should guarantee that such success will not be at the crippling expense of existing carriers in the region.

"On the basis of the foregoing facts and all of the facts of record, it is concluded that Atlantic is fit, willing and able to perform the operations it proposes, and that the public convenience and necessity require the temporary certification of Atlantic for certain routes . . . for the purpose of determining whether air transportation can economically be extended to broader sections of the public independently of governmental aid."

There was elation at Atlantic's Carlton headquarters but Sam Solomon knew that the battle was far from won. The recommendation had to be reviewed and acted upon by the full Civil Aeronautics Board, and the Board had often been known to overturn an Examiner's finding. Now that the report had been made public, Atlantic could look for even stronger pressure from the certificated airlines, and despite the heartening substance of the Examiner's statement, a knowledgeable oddsmaker would have given Atlantic no better than an even chance.

As was the custom, Sam filed a brief with the CAB commenting upon the Examiner's recommendation and offering additional justification for Atlantic's certification. Then he sat back to await the final decision.

It was during this period that Sam helped form a unique social group. It started when he and Alma invited some 20 couples to their Silver Spring home for a Sunday evening gathering. From that first meeting sprang the Sunday Night Club, which convened fortnightly at the homes of the members on a rotating-host basis. The host—and/or hostess—was responsible for providing light refreshments and a program, usually a speaker or an entertainer. The unique part—at least unique for postwar Washington—was the club's simple dictum: 'No politics, no alcohol, home by 10." The club was successful from the beginning, amazingly so in Sam's estimation. The restriction on politics and the lack of alcohol never tongue-tied the interesting collection of members and guests, many of whom were nationally prominent. The Sunday Night Club continued in existence for over six years.

In September, 1947, Sam Solomon became affiliated with TACA, the international airline he had earlier been asked to head. In the wake of the departure of Jack Frye and Ben Pepper, Waterman Steamship Company had acquired control of TACA and named Paul Richter, former executive vice president of TWA, its president. Richter asked Sam to serve on the board and Sam assented; he was to continue as a TACA director for eight years.

Shortly after he joined the TACA board, Sam acquired another part-time connection, as consultant to a group of ship operators. The subsidized steamship passenger lines of the United States had formed the Sea-Air Committee to explore the possibilities of moving into the air transportation field. Tirey L. Ford, chairman of the committee, approached Solomon and invited him to be advisor to the group.

Sam felt there was little he could do for the steamship people.

From his experience of a few years earlier, when the railroad partners in Northeast Airlines had been forced to reduce their stock holdings, he was thoroughly familiar with the CAB's attitude concerning control of airlines by non-aviation transportation firms.

Back in 1940, the CAB had granted a certificate authorizing American Export Airlines, a subsidiary of a steamship company, American Export Lines, to operate across the Atlantic. Pan American Airways, which had strenuously opposed the application, took the case to the U.S. Circuit Court of Appeals, which ruled that the CAB should reconsider. On second look, the CAB decided that the parent steamship company would have to relinquish control of the airline if the airline was to continue in business.

That attitude still prevailed and Sam so advised Ford, adding that he saw no way in which the shipping people could operate airlines. Therefore, his services would be of little use to the Sea-Air Committee. Nonetheless, Ford said, he would like to retain Sam as consultant.

"I couldn't do it for less than a thousand a month," Sam said, thinking that the figure would bring an abrupt end to Ford's interest.

"That's not good enough," Ford countered. "How about fifteen hundred?"

If they wanted him that badly, Sam reasoned, why fight it? So he accepted the post, in which he was to serve for some three years. His duties did not take much of his time; he attended meetings whenever they were held and, when called upon, reiterated his original advice: that authorization for steamship companies to operate air services would not be forthcoming unless there was a dramatic change in governmental attitudes.

Eventually, tiring of the monotony of his counsel, Sam tendered his resignation. As a parting remembrance, the committee presented him a beautiful, exquisitely-detailed yard-long model of the *Flying Cloud*, the famous 19th century clipper ship. Soon after Solomon's withdrawal, the Sea-Air Committee recognized the futility of its effort and disbanded.

While the Civil Aeronautics Board was deliberating the final outcome of the Middle Atlantic Case, Atlantic Airlines was engaged in another program. Sam Solomon, who had been a helicopter enthusiast ever since he witnessed the Sikorsky demonstration several years earlier, began thinking in terms of rotary-wing mail and passenger service. No one in the industry had yet taken a comprehensive look at the commercial potential of the helicopter, so Sam initiated another "first." He assigned David Morrow, the engineer who had designed the integral loading stairs, to make a detailed study of "The Helicopter and Its Commercial Operation."

Assisted by other Atlantic staffers, Morrow interviewed representatives of all the American helicopter builders and came up with a fine report which detailed the status of existing helicopters, what new types could be expected in the near and distant future, operating costs and other problems, and concluded with an analysis of helicopter mail and passenger service over selected routes. The report was made available to the industry and neither Sam nor Atlantic ever realized any gain from it. However, being the first of its kind, the study made a valuable contribution to the progress of American air transportation; it inspired further examinations of the potential of the helicopter, which was introduced to commercial service a few years later.

Late in 1947, Sam Solomon was again asked to serve the military. The U.S. Air Force, now an independent service and no longer a branch of the Army, was reorganizing its Reserve forces in the wake of World War II. The Air Transport Command requested that Solomon form a committee to study the specialized mobilization requirements of the Command in the event of a future emergency, and to recommend a program whereby ATC could train and maintain a peacetime Reserve of skilled flight and ground personnel.

Sam assembled a group that included Jerome Lederer, his principal aide during the period when he had directed the activities of the Airlines War Training Institute; Walter Hartung of the Casey Jones School of Aeronautics; Dallas Sherman of Pan American; and Grove Webster, who had been active in the Civilian Pilot Training Program.

Operating from Sam's Carlton office, the committee spent several months putting together detailed recommendations as to how the ATC Reserve program should be effected. It was, the military agreed, an excellent report but the project ended on a flat note. The Department of Defense had decreed that the Air Transport Command and the Naval Air Transport Service be merged into a single Military Air Transport Service. In the hectic process of coupling an Air Force command with a Navy command, the problems of training Reserves were deferred and the committee's report was buried under a mound of more pressing business. Although many of the committee's recommendations were later put into effect, neither Sam nor his teammates ever received any formal recognition. Which was all right with Sam Solomon, who was personally satisfied that he had made still another contribution to the military and that recognition—or lack of it—was not important.

On April 6, 1948, the CAB's axe fell on Atlantic Airlines. The Board issued its final decision in the Middle Atlantic Case, denying Sam Solomon's application for route authorizations. To Sam, it was not a surprising development; he had been aware for some time that the intense pressure exerted by the certificated airlines was taking effect. Nonetheless, it was a bitter disappointment to him, his Atlantic Airlines staff and other champions of the coach concept.

The Board's decision was popular only with the scheduled airlines. From other sources came a flurry of editorial protest. For example, pioneer flyer Al Williams wrote in his syndicated column:

"Sam Solomon knows his air business and has successfully handled several large aviation projects. No one on the Civil Aeronautics Board knows much about any phase of aviation beyond what he picked up while serving on that Board. Certainly no CAB member has had any airline operation experience, neither has he managed any major aviation business.

"The government, in this case the CAB, has refused to grant Solomon a permit to operate his aerial bus line, offering its own inexperienced opinion that Solomon's operation cost estimates are too low. 'Too low by what yardstick?' asks Solomon.

"With the government dominating business in this fashion, Thomas Edison would never have been permitted to raise funds for building and selling electric power or electric lights. I doubt whether Henry Ford would have been granted a license to demonstrate his first Model T Ford."

The protests, of course, availed nothing; the decision stuck. And there came in the immediate wake of the Board's report an ironic development: Capital Airlines, which had strongly opposed the coach concept during CAB hearings, instituted the first air coach service. It was an instant success; as Sam Solomon had predicted, the traveling public was very much interested in frill-less, lower fare service and early returns indicated that the coach concept was, in fact, attracting passengers who had never flown before. Jolted into action by Capital's success, the other major airlines—with the exception of United, which held out for years—began laying plans for coach services of their own.

The "Father of the Air Coach," as some publications had dubbed Sam Solomon, smiled wistfully as coach travel burgeoned. Shortly after the CAB had rendered its decision, he had filed for reconsideration through the U.S. Circuit Court of Appeals; now he withdrew the appeal before it reached the hearing stage.

"The time has gone by," he said; with most of the certificated airlines preparing to introduce low-fare service, the Board could validly argue that there was no longer a need for a new coach carrier.

At the end of 1948, Sam Solomon distributed the remaining capital of Atlantic Airlines among the stockholders and closed shop. He accepted his defeat philosophically. It was a defeat, he reasoned, only in the sense that he had not been allowed to follow through on his own concept. There was no doubt, however, that his application and the wide publicity it engendered had been a prime factor in the birth of air coach service. He foresaw — accurately, as it proved—that in years to come low-fare operations would expand enormously, attracting more and more first-time customers, eventually reaching the point where coach and other economy services would completely dominate commercial air transportation. Not only the traveling public, but even the airlines which had so vigorously fought the innovation would benefit from the tremendously broadened market.

Though Sam had been personally stymied by the Board's action, he had nonetheless led the parade once again in a vital area of air transport progress. There were many who acknowledged, publicly and privately, Sam Solomon's contribution. One of them was J. H. "Slim" Carmichael, president of Capital Airlines, whose company was reaping both financial and prestigial rewards from its introduction of air coach service.

"Sam," said Carmichael, "they're pinning medals on me for something that you created."

CHAPTER XII

Another War, Another Training Assignment

For several months after the demise of Atlantic Airlines, Sam Solomon was practically unemployed. For a man who had spent most of his life on a multiple job basis, it was a strange and surprisingly pleasant condition.

At about the time he had disbanded the airline, Sam had also divested himself of his interest in Harris Motors, the Norfolk auto sales agency. Sam had discovered that he was temperamentally unsuited to the role of absentee owner; if he was to be part of an enterprise, then he had to jump in, learn all about it and try to find ways to make it a more efficient operation. This he did, but the frequent trips to Norfolk were time-consuming and not particularly rewarding; selling automobiles, he found, lacked the excitement and uplift of running an airline. So he sold his share of the agency to Vince Conroy, one of his associates in the Atlantic Airlines venture, and exited the auto business.

From the first of the year into the late summer of 1949, Sam had no full-time occupation and only light part-time duties. He was still a director of TACA and he attended the airline's board meetings, and he also made his appearance at the infrequent sessions of the Sea-Air Committee. In addition, he served on occasion as a consultant to aviation firms. In one such connection, he helped Roscoe Turner, the famous and colorful racing pilot, in the formation of a small feeder line which later evolved into Lake Central Airlines.

For the most part, though, Sam enjoyed a life of unaccustomed leisure, socializing with friends, working out at the YMCA or playing golf at Argyle Country Club near his Silver Spring home where he held the Number One membership card. From time to time he felt the urge to plunge again into airline operation and no doubt his acknowledged expertise would have been welcomed by several companies had he actively sought a position. But, now turning 50 and in good financial status by virtue of the sale of his Northeast stock, Sam was in no great hurry to offer his services. If the right job came along . . . . .

It came, in August of 1949, when Andre de Saint-Phalle and Neil Berboth, president and vice president respectively of California-Eastern Airways, paid him a visit in Washington. Cal-Eastern maintained a headquarters office in New York and a flight operations center in Oakland, California.

Saint-Phalle outlined his company's situation. At the end of World War II, Cal-Eastern had gone into the air freight haulage business, operating four four-engine Douglas DC-4s. Although air freight was later to become a booming business, the nation had not been ready for it in the immediate postwar years. The company had lost money from the start and had wound up in receivership.

Under Chapter 11 of the Bankruptcy Act, by which the court may permit a bankrupt firm to remain in business if a majority of the creditors concur, Cal-Eastern was still conducting limited operations. It was no longer handling freight but it was leasing its airplanes to other operators and gaining additional income by providing maintenance services for its own leased DC-4s and for other aircraft.

Now, Saint-Phalle said, the company was hoping to resume flying its own airplanes, but in passenger rather than freight service. Cal-Eastern had retained Coudert Brothers, one of New York's foremost legal firms, to draw up an application for transcontinental air coach operations. The application had already been filed with the Civil Aeronautics Board.

"We feel," Saint-Phalle told Solomon, "that you know more about air coach than anyone in the country. We want you with us. We can offer you the presidency of the company." As president, Sam learned, he would actually be second in command; Saint-Phalle would retain his status as chief executive officer. Sam's job would be to spearhead the CAB hearings and, if the application was approved, to set up and direct the air coach operation.

Sam liked the sound of the proposition, but he asked for time to think about it. He was, on the one hand, reluctant to abandon his new-found freedom. But he was still a long way from the customary retirement age and there was no equally attractive opportunity on the horizon. Sam still firmly believed in the public need for expanded air coach services, but having just been through the CAB mill he entertained some doubts as to whether the Cal-Eastern application would be successful.

There were, however, a couple of factors which seemed to give Cal-Eastern a better chance than Atlantic Airlines had had. For one thing, Cal-Eastern was an operating entity with some experience in hauling passengers on a charter basis. For another, where the CAB had challenged Atlantic Airlines' presentations with regard to air coach economics, the scheduled airlines were already demonstrating that low-fare transportation could be operated with a profit.

The airlines, however, had not plunged full-tilt into coach service; the traditional attitude still prevailed that air transportation, because of the speed and convenience it offered, warranted a premium fare. Only a few airlines were experimenting with coach operations and they were flying infrequent coach schedules, sometimes in the middle of the night to take advantage of the hours during which their airplanes would otherwise be idle. Sam felt that the CAB might now be in a mood to consider favorably an application for regularly-scheduled, all-coach, coast-to-coast service.

The thing that tipped the balance in favor of Sam's acceptance was the fact that Cal-Eastern was bankrupt. Sam Solomon had once been bankrupt; he still remembered, and he would remember all his life, the humiliation of that experience and the long, tough struggle to pay off every cent of his indebtedness. Andre de Saint-Phalle had pledged, with obvious sincerity, that he would somehow find ways of clearing Cal-Eastern's debts. Sam wanted to help him do it.

After several days of deliberation, Sam decided to sacrifice his leisure to the thrill of new challenge and he notified Saint-Phalle that he would accept the Cal-Eastern post.

In September, 1949, at a meeting of the company's stockholders in Oakland, Sam Solomon was elected president of California-Eastern Airways. Andre de Saint-Phalle was to continue as chief executive officer and he was additionally named chairman of the board. R. E. Caskey was re-elected vice president and general manager in charge of the company's flight activities at Oakland. Sam had made it a proviso of his acceptance that he be allowed to operate from Washington, because his major responsibility would be monitoring the CAB procedure, so once again the world's leading commuter took to the road with a visit to the New York office about once a week and less frequent trips to the Oakland facility.

While the Cal-Eastern coach application wound its slow way through the CAB mechanism, there came an international development which was to effect a complete change of course in the company's direction. On June 25, 1950, the Communist forces of North Korea, officially known as the Democratic People's Republic of Korea, invaded anti-Communist, U.S.-backed South Korea. The United Nations immediately authorized its member nations to support South Korea and the main burden of defense fell to the United States, leader of the free world. Thus, less than five years after the end of World War II, the United States found itself embroiled in another major conflict. The nation was ill-prepared for the task. Satisfied that it had, in 1945, defeated the forces of aggression once and for all, the U.S. had been busy dismantling its war machine. The Air Force had been particularly hard hit in the demobilization process; from an overall strength of more than 250 groups in World War II, it had declined by 1950 to a force less than one-fifth that size.

Among shortages of everything, one of the most pressing needs was an increase in the Air Force's transport capability. General Douglas MacArthur, Supreme Commander Allied Powers, called for immediate activation of a priority air lift for the transport of men and equipment from the United States to Japan, the staging area for Korean operations. But the Military Air Transport Service could assign only 60 four-engine transports of sufficient range to cross the Pacific on the longest aerial supply line in history.

It was not enough. Once again the production lines started rolling, but it would be a year or more before the first new airplanes were available. The war couldn't wait. As it had in World War II, the Air Force again sought help from the airlines.

As soon as he heard that the USAF was looking for commercial contractors, Sam prepared a Cal-Eastern prospectus and took it to Air Force headquarters in the Pentagon. There he met with Colonel Win Long, an air staff transportation officer, and outlined his company's capabilities: it had transport aircraft, it had the crews to fly them and it had an established West Coast maintenance base for servicing its own planes and those of other contractors. As Sam learned later, it was not the company's capabilities but his own that impressed the Air Force; the people in charge of selecting commercial operators for the lift were aware of Northeast Airlines' World War II performance and the part Sam Solomon had played in it. Cal-Eastern became one of the first of the 17 commercial companies awarded contracts.

On August 6, 1950, Cal-Eastern flew its inaugural mission on the Pacific Air Lift, departing Travis Air Force Base, California, the primary Stateside terminal, bound for Tokyo via Hawaii and Wake Island. From then on Cal-Eastern's DC-4's were in continual service on the military lift, shuttling back and forth across the Pacific with troops and vital supplies. The locale was different, the planes were different, he was part of a different company, but to Sam Solomon it was Northeast Airlines and the North Atlantic aerial pipe-line all over again.

The Korean war had a second and even greater influence—from the standpoint of effort involved—on Cal-Eastern. With the outbreak of hostilities, the Department of Defense ordered an Air Force expansion from 48 to 95 combat groups. This required training of 7,200 new pilots a year. But in 1950 the Air Training Command was turning out only slightly more than 2,000 pilots annually.

The Air Force started a large-scale recruiting program and tried desperately to step up its pilot output. However, the few existing training schools soon became overcrowded, the number of instructors available was insufficient and the flow of trainees bottlenecked.

Late in 1950, the USAF came up with a new plan: the Air Force would use its own instructors and facilities for advanced pilot training; the primary, or initial phase of instruction would be contracted to civilian schools. Each contractor would be assigned a base, newly-activated from among the supply of disused World War II facilities. The base would be staffed by a USAF unit, which would handle drilling, medical and religious matters. Everything else—training, the provision of instructors, aircraft maintenance, base maintenance, water and sewage disposal systems, housing and feeding of the trainees—would be the civilian firm's responsibility.

The Air Force began asking for bids from civilian schools with which it had done business in the past. Andre de Saint-Phalle got wind of the program and immediately called Sam Solomon, who entered a bid in behalf of California-Eastern Airways. All of the other bidders boasted existing schools, instructor staffs and World War II records of service. Cal-Eastern had none of these assets, but it had Sam Solomon, former president of the Airlines War Training Institute and as such director of the entire World War II contract training program. More recently, Sam had headed the committee which had advised the Air Transport Command as to techniques for peacetime Reserve training.

By a happy coincidence, the man who had sought Sam's assistance on the Air Transport Command Reserve matter was now the commander of Air Training Command—Lieutenant General Robert W. Harper. Following up Cal-Eastern's bid for a contract, Sam visited Harper and persuasively set forth his own and his company's qualifications. The latter were slim—considerable experience in maintenance but no background in flight training—but once again Sam's own reputation and expertise tipped the scales. Early in 1951, Cal-Eastern was notified that the Air Force had accepted its bid and that the company would be assigned a training facility at Columbus Air Force Base, Mississippi.

Because of his long familiarity with training matters, Cal-Eastern designated Sam Solomon director of a newly-formed Training Division in addition to his other duties. Sam's first need for the Columbus operation was a resident assistant director who would live full time at the base and manage the training program while Sam would handle overall supervision, commuting frequently to the base from his home in Silver Spring. He found one, an old acquaintance: Ben Cole, who had once headed Northeast's training school and who had later served as a vice president of Atlantic Airlines. Cole was a valuable acquisition; he had a talent for organization and he was eminently qualified as a training director. Cole immediately began recruiting flight instructors, maintenance technicians and management people.

On February 1, 1952, Cal-Eastern took over Columbus AFB and almost immediately started training the first class of cadets.

Sam, who was provided a home on the air base for the frequent visits he would be required to make, enjoyed unique status at Columbus. As program director, he was a civilian boss of a military installation. An Air Force officer—Lieutenant Colonel Bruce Palmer—was commanding officer of the base as regards military activities and discipline but Sam Solomon was top man in everything connected with the training operation.

As president of a company which had suddenly become one of Columbus' largest industries, Sam also undertook direction of a community relations program, assisted by Alma Solomon, who accompanied her husband on many of his visits to the base.

A major community relations problem resulted from the fact that liquor was available, by the drink or by the bottle, at the base officers' club. Mississippi was technically speaking a dry state, but no one took the law very seriously. Thirsty locals were able to find a number of spas whose proprietors winked at the law; some even posted signs advertising the availability of hard liquor.

Nonetheless, the officers' club became one of the area's most popular oases. By Air Force regulation, reserve officers not on active duty were entitled to the use of USAF clubs and there was a substantial group of reservists in the neighborhood. They were in nightly attendance at the bar and they frequently used the club for dinner parties or other gatherings. Sam considered this a community relations asset; it gave him and the other base people an opportunity to become well acquainted with a large segment of the local populace.

However, some of the citizenry didn't like the idea and protested it, through the local sheriff to Air Training Command headquarters. Sam never learned the identity of the complainers—quite possibly they were bar operators who were losing business—but the result was an order from Air Training Command to the effect that all liquor sales, to base personnel as well as reservists, would cease forthwith. Sam was advised informally that the order would be cancelled if the sheriff could be persuaded to reverse his position.

Sam went to see the sheriff and argued that it was unfair to deny liquor to the officers club when it was so readily available elsewhere. He acquainted the sheriff with the fact that club patronage by the reservist townspeople served a community relations purpose. The sheriff, a reasonable man, saw the light and agreed to withdraw his objection in the interests of better base-community rapport. In due time, Air Training Command informally permitted Sam to reopen the bar. What had started out as a problem ended up a benefit because Sam's championship of the cause elevated his status in the estimation of the Columbians.

Cal-Eastern and the Air Force cooperated on construction of a 9-hole golf course at Columbus AFB. When completed, it turned out to be a fine course with one notable exception—on one hole there was a huge tree smack in the middle of the fairway and it took more skill than most of the Columbus golfers possessed to negotiate it. There were a number of complaints and Sam Solomon, who played the course as often as his busy schedule would permit, was one of those who favored removal of the tree. But Bruce Palmer, apparently a nature lover, couldn't bring himself to destroy the great tree; as base housekeeper, he had the final word and the tree remained.

Until one day when a visiting general officer from Air Training Command made an inspection tour of the base and took time off to try the golf course. Playing with Sam, the general reached the controversial hole and hit a respectable tee shot which, unfortunately, ended up directly behind the tree.

"What's that goddam tree doing in the middle of the fairway?" the general grumbled.

Sam shrugged and replied that it was an Air Force matter, not a training responsibility.

The next day, after the general departed, workmen were busy taking down the tree.

With the golf course in full operation, Sam decided that there was a need for a golf shop where base personnel could buy balls, clubs and other accessories of the game. He contacted Wilson Sporting Goods Company, which sent a representative to Columbus AFB to look over the layout and decide whether the base club warranted a sales agency.

The decision was negative. It was a nice course, the Wilson man told Sam and Billy Vaughn, the Base Exchange manager who was sitting in on the discussion, but there was a problem.

"We can't license you to sell our top-line equipment," said the man from Wilson, "because our company rules require that you have a golf professional at the club. You don't have one."

Sam made a command decision.

"We certainly do," he stated.

"Who is he?"

"Him." Sam pointed at a surprised Billy Vaughn. "He has just been appointed golf pro."

The Wilson man smiled and, with a little additional arm-twisting agreed to put in the concession. But the solution to one problem brought another. Once he got used to the idea of being a golf pro, Billy Vaughn began to take his assignment seriously. Every day, for long hours at a time, he could be found on the course sharpening his golf; if he was going to have the name he must have the game to go with it. As a result, the Base Exchange almost foundered, its manager too busy with his new career to attend to routine business.

On February 10, 1952, Columbus Air Force Base marked its first anniversary under Cal-Eastern management. It had been a very good year. Starting from scratch, Solomon, Cole and others of the Cal-Eastern team had created a smoothly functioning training operation that the Air Force regarded as one of its best. The base population now numbered 2,000 people, including trainees and military cadre; almost half of that number were Cal-Eastern employees—management people, instructors and other flight operations personnel, maintenance men and a variety of supporting workers. In its first year, the base had graduated and sent on to advanced training some 700 USAF pilots and about 60 others from foreign nations participating in the Mutual Defense Assistance Program.

In the interim, there had been developments on other Cal-Eastern fronts. The long-pending application to the Civil Aeronautics Board for coach service had been denied. The decision came as no surprise; in the period during which the application was being considered, more and more certificated airlines had started air coach operations. It was not in the cards for the CAB to authorize a new service at a time when the existing airlines were demonstrating their willingness to meet the public need for lower-fare transportation. The turndown was not much of a blow to Cal-Eastern, which was fully occupied with its military commitments.

The combination of incomes from the Pacific air lift, the Columbus training program and a number of new contracts for maintenance of civil aircraft had effected a marked change in Cal-Eastern's financial position. The company had been able to pay off its creditors and get out of receivership, an achievement which brought both Andre de Saint-Phalle and Sam Solomon great personal satisfaction. Saint-Phalle had been dedicated to that goal and the accomplishment of it had been due in great measure to his efficient management of the firm. As for Sam, there was no doubt that his reputation with the Air Force had been the principle factor in Cal-Eastern's acquisition of military contracts. That, in turn, had been the major contributor to the company's extrication from its financial morass.

Once again solvent, Cal-Eastern embarked upon an expansion program, broadening its areas of interest with the acquisition of two subsidiaries. One of them was Land-Air, Inc., a new firm engaged in manufacture of electronic equipment and provision of electronic engineering services. The other was Air Carrier Service Corporation, which maintained sales representation and advisory services for airlines all over the world. Land-Air was based in Chicago; Air Carrier Service Corporation was headquartered in Washington.

Although he was now essentially a one-job man, Sam Solomon was traveling almost as much as he had in the hectic, multiple-occupation years of World War II. In addition to his regular visits to Cal-Eastern's New York headquarters and to Columbus Air Force Base, Sam flew the Pacific air lift in company aircraft on a number of occasions to acquire first-hand knowledge of the long-distance supply operation. He made several trips to Hawaii, the first leg of the trans-Pacific route, and twice went all the way to Tokyo. On the first trip, which took place during the early days of Cal-Eastern's Pacific service, Sam squeezed into a cabin loaded from floor to ceiling with cargo. With no place to sit, he was forced to make the seemingly interminable journey stretched out atop an auxiliary fuel tank. It brought reminiscences of an earlier experience when, clad in a tropical suit, he had shared a cabin with a cargo load on Northeast Airlines' initial flight across the North Atlantic.

Sam missed the anniversary celebration at Columbus because it coincided with his second visit to Tokyo. On that occasion, he was accompanied by his wife Alma, who struck a blow for the uplift of women's status in Japan. The Solomons were invited to a dinner party attended by a number of Japanese businessmen and Alma found herself the sole female in the gathering.

"Where are your wives?" she asked, "I want to meet them." By Japanese custom, wives did not normally attend such functions, it was explained, but the men of Nippon graciously bowed to the wish of their Western guest. At a similar party the following evening, several of the wives were present, pleased at their unaccustomed exposure to social life.

It was during this second visit to Tokyo that Sam Solomon laid the groundwork for an agreement whereby Cal-Eastern would team with a Japanese group on a projected joint international airline venture.

In the years of American occupation following the end of World War II, Japan had not been allowed to operate heavy aircraft, including airliners. In 1951, however, restrictions were eased and in August of that year the United States permitted Japan to start a domestic air transport service operated by Japan Air Lines. Now, in 1952, with ratification of the U.S.-Japanese Peace Treaty expected within a few months, Japan had ambitions of inaugurating international service. Japan Air Lines wanted the franchise. So did another group, headed by officials of Osaka Shosen Kaisha, Japan's largest shipping company.

The latter group had made contact with Cal-Eastern through Ernest Silver, Tokyo representative of the company's subsidiary, Air Carrier Service Corporation. Japan had no aircraft manufacturing industry, so the group planned to employ American planes. The only flight crews qualified for transport operations were working for Japan Air Lines, so the competing group needed American crews and American instructors to train Japanese pilots. The OSK group also needed American know-how for long overwater flights; it sought to contract with an American carrier for all these requirements.

For Sam Solomon, it offered an opportunity to participate in the development of an international airline, an old dream. With the concurrence of the Cal-Eastern board, he and Saint-Phalle worked out an agreement with the Japanese shipping firm. The company, to be known as Japan International World Airlines, would seek a route via the Pacific islands to San Francisco, thence to Mexico and Panama, and from there by way of intermediate stops to Rio de Janeiro, Brazil. In Brazil there was a large Japanese colony which could be expected to supply some return traffic to Tokyo in addition to attracting Japanese visitors to South America.

Under the agreement, Cal-Eastern would supply the airplanes, flight crews, maintenance, communications facilities and dispatch services. Additionally, it would undertake to train Japanese flight and ground personnel for later employment. OSK would provide financing and set up international traffic offices. The agreement, of course, was subject to approval by the Japanese government once the peace treaty was ratified, and also to landing rights authorizations from the other governments involved. There would be a wait of some 18 months before the Japanese government could be expected to make a decision; in the meantime, representatives of JIWA and Cal-Eastern would iron out the operating details of the projected airline.

In July, 1952, Sam Solomon accepted a Department of Defense invitation to attend one of the indoctrination tours DOD frequently sponsored to acquaint civilian "opinion leaders" with military operations. This one involved a trip aboard an aircraft carrier cruising in the Pacific. It was an interesting and enjoyable experience, but Sam's tour was cut short by a cable from Air Training Command, directing him to report to the contracting officer at Forth Worth, Texas. Sam left the tour, flew to Fort Worth and checked into a hotel the night before the stated time of the meeting, completely mystified as to the reason for his summons. He dined at a local restaurant and unexpectedly ran into an old acquaintance, Colonel Bill McDuffie.

"What are you doing here?" Sam asked.

"I," McDuffie replied, "am the guy you're here to meet."

Air Training Command, McDuffie explained, had called a conference to acquaint the training directors of the various civilian-operated primary training schools with a planned change in procedure; beyond that he would not comment.

At the conference the following day, conducted by McDuffie and other USAF contract officers, it turned out that there was little reason for all the secrecy, other than a possible public relations influence. The new plan was about as secret as the weather report. It involved simply a change in the types of aircraft used for primary training. The USAF had been using the relatively large, 600-horsepower T-6, which during World War II had been employed as an advanced trainer. The Air Force was finding that novice fliers, with no previous experience, were having difficulty handling the big trainer. There was a need for a small lightplane for initial flight familiarization, after which the trainees could make an easy transition to the T-6.

The public relations matter stemmed from the manner in which the USAF planned to handle procurement of the new lightplane trainers. The civilian school operators were advised that, although the USAF would fund the purchases, the airplanes were to be bought by the contracting firms so that they would not be reflected in the Air Force inventory. No reason was stated, but apparently it was a move designed to block critics of the air power build-up, who challenged the need for the large numbers of aircraft the USAF was buying. These critics invariably cited overall annual purchases, which included trainers, helicopters and utility airplanes, types which had no bearing on combat strength. More than 240 lightplanes were involved in the new plan and that figure, lumped in with the Air Force's procurement of fighters and bombers, might give the public an erroneous impression of true combat capability and have an effect on future appropriations.

To simplify the purchase of the lightplanes, a briefing officer stated, a single school operator would negotiate a contract on behalf of all the schools. Air Training Command had already selected the man for the job—Samuel J. Solomon. Sam, who had had no inkling of his new assignment was surprised and not particularly enthusiastic, but he made no objection.

After the conference, Sam was sought out by Colonel William Reynolds, the Air Training Command coordinator for the civilian flying schools. There would be no need for a lengthy evaluation of the available lightplanes, Reynolds told Sam, because the Air Force had already decided upon the type it wanted—the Piper Cub.

"Wait a minute," Sam objected. "If you want me to buy these airplanes, we'll do it on an advertised bid basis."

"There's no need," the colonel argued. "We already know what we want."

"Then you buy them, or get somebody else. If you want me to do it, we'll ask for bids."

The colonel conceded and Sam solicited bids from the seven major lightplane producers. Five of them responded. As it turned out, Piper Aircraft was not only the lowest bidder, its Cub was the best airplane in other respects; but at least Sam had the satisfaction of knowing that he had conducted a proper evaluation. He negotiated a contract with Piper calling for delivery of 243 of the airplanes at a cost of $827,000.

Sam's unwanted assignment as purchasing agent proved to be a continuing headache. No sooner had the Piper contract been announced than a United States Senator landed on Sam with both feet; why, the Senator wanted to know, had one of his constituents not been invited to bid? On investigation, Sam found that in the Senator's state there was a small firm building an experimental lightplane, but even if the plane met the specifications—which it could not—the company had no facilities for production in the required numbers. Nonetheless, the Senator suspected chicanery and threatened a Congressional investigation.

"Listen," Sam replied, "I'd welcome an investigation. I'd get to spend some time in Washington." The matter went no further.

Then, Sam found, his job had not ended with the signing of the contract; he would have to supervise deliveries and acceptances, which would involve him in paper work for several months, well into 1953. And if that weren't enough, he would also have to oversee future engine overhauls. As far as the Air Force was concerned, the 243 Cubs were Sam Solomon's airplanes, and it would be his responsibility to negotiate contracts for overhauls even after the planes were in service with 10 schools other than his own. Sam was to remain Custodian of the Cubs for several years.

In July, 1953, the Korean war came to an end and with the cessation of hostilities Cal-Eastern's Pacific air lift contract was cancelled. Only temporarily, however. The Department of Defense soon found that it had been too hasty in suspending the lift. American troops were to remain in Korea for several years and their support, together with the dictates of South Korean readjustment, required continuing aerial supply movement, though at a reduced level. Cal-Eastern was one of the airlines invited to resume its lift operations.

The plan to participate in the international airline venture with the Japanese shipping company fell through in August, 1953. After months of deliberations, the Japanese government had decided the manner in which it would structure its international airline. It would adopt the "chosen instrument" concept, long ago rejected in the United States. There would be a single overseas air transportation company in which the government would acquire the majority of the stock in exchange for financing. Both Japan Air Lines and Japan International World Airlines would be allowed minority shareholdings, but Japan Air Lines was to be the operating entity. The Japanese would buy their own airplanes, so Cal-Eastern's agreement with JIWA was voided.

On the home front, Sam Solomon lost the services of his long time associate, the resident director at Columbus Air Force Base, Ben Cole. Cole, recalcitrant as ever, had never liked the Air Force way of doing things. After more than two years of constant argument with USAF brass, he resigned. He was succeeded by J. Dudley Watson, a local education specialist who had no aviation background but was regarded as a top-grade program manager.

Early in 1954, the school began its fourth year under Cal-Eastern's aegis. Despite the loss of Cole, it was operating with exceptional efficiency. It had turned out more than 2,000 primary-trained pilots and it boasted a proud record of flight safety. But, at mid-year, came a problem.

Columbus was a big base, some 12,000 acres, far more than was needed for a primary training facility. The Air Force's Strategic Air Command, looking for elbow room for its expanding operations, cast a greedy eye upon Columbus. SAC, the major combat command, enjoyed top priority within the Air Force and it got the base. The Air Force ordered Cal-Eastern to move its school to Moore Air Base in Mission, Texas.

It was a massive headache. Moore had been a World War II training base but it had been inactive for years. Such buildings as were usable had to be rehabilitated; a lot of new construction was required. The disused runways had to be repaired. Cal-Eastern's civilian employees and their families had to be moved from Mississippi to Texas. Some of them—about half—elected not to go;

this necessitated a new recruiting program. The Air Force generously allowed Cal-Eastern six months to take care of these and other preliminaries, but added that training must continue without interruption at Columbus until Moore Air Base was ready to open its doors for business. On July 1, 1954, Sam Solomon and his Cal-Eastern team began work on the problem-packed transition.

CHAPTER XIII

The National Aviation Club

Washington, D. C. has long been the focal point of American aviation. All of the government agencies involved in either civil or military air matters are headquartered there and as a consequence more aviation business is transacted in the Capital than anywhere else in the nation. Although their corporate offices are located elsewhere, every major airline and aircraft manufacturing company maintains a Washington branch. In addition, there are the representatives of the smaller air carriers, aircraft component producers, air publications, private consulting firms, trade associations, societies and foundations. On top of that, there is a large and constant flow of out-of-towners who must on frequent occasion visit the government officials with whom they are doing business.

For years these people had felt the need for a central meeting place where they could gather with others in their field to exchange views, swap rumors, find out what a competitor was up to or simply relax with a tall glass after a hard day's combat at the Pentagon or the CAB. There had been a lot of talk about starting a club and even one abortive effort to lease a facility, but until 1954 the club failed to materialize. Then, suddenly, it sprang into being and naturally Sam Solomon was in the thick of the action.

Through a friend, Sam had been invited to serve on the board of another club, a non-aviation organization. Sam agreed to look into it and arrived at the club one day just in time to mourn at its wake; the club was going bankrupt and was about to suspend operations.

Sam took a look at the club's quarters anyway. It was a large brownstone building at the corner of 19th and R Streets, built decades earlier as a private residence. Its interior design left a lot to be desired from the standpoint of club function and it was off the paths usually beaten by aviation folk. But, soon to be vacated, it had the attraction of availability; it might serve at least as an interim home for the long-awaited aviation club.

Sam discussed his find with three close friends: Howard Rough, a longtime aviation man then retired; Barney Vierling of Aircraft Supply Company; and Richard E. Fell, a former Air Force colonel who was running a service and maintenance facility at Washington National Airport. Together the foursome took another look at the building and made the plunge, renting the old brownstone and forming the Washington Aviation Club, which later became the National Aero Club and finally the National Aviation Club. Rough became president, Vierling vice president, Fell secretary-treasurer and Sam Solomon chairman of the executive committee.

The first need was for enough members to support the operation. The founding foursome went about collaring every friend and acquaintance in bars, restaurants and even in the streets. Sam Solomon had a particularly effective technique.

"Give me sixty dollars," he would demand. The surprised victim, perhaps thinking that Sam needed a loan, would reach for his checkbook. Then he would be informed that he had just paid his first year's dues in the National Aviation Club.

Sam Solomon came up with a new wrinkle—the corporate membership. It happened that the club needed $300 on a "right now" basis, to meet some pressing debts, so Sam invented the corporate plan whereby for $300 a company could name 10 members. This, of course, was only half the individual membership rate, but what the fledgling club needed most was bodies. Sam took out the first corporate membership for his own company, thereby meeting the immediate need for $300. A number of other firms followed Sam's lead, providing considerable impetus to the membership drive.

In the early days, club operation was haphazard. There was meal service of a sort and no one ever went thirsty but beverage service was a random thing. The club had no liquor license, a fact which the District authorities never discovered and which the founders were willing to overlook. Operating expenses ate up most of the dues income and there was not enough left over to build up a large bar stock. So, almost daily, one of the officers would give Louie the bartender some money and send him to the nearby liquor store for a short-term stock.

Members did not exactly flock to the club, but there was a slow, steady growth. After the first year's operation, it became apparent that the club's quarters were no longer adequate; there was plenty of room in the old, four-story manse but it was the wrong kind of room. Club officials began to look for a new facility.

To acquire one, some working capital was needed. One of the early members, Richard S. Boutelle, president of Fairchild Engine and Airplane Corporation, spearheaded a fund-raising drive. He sought—and obtained from several sources, including his own company—loans ranging from $1,000 to $5,000, to be repaid when the club started to realize some income. The drive produced some $37,000.

Thus bolstered financially, the club elevated its sights and initiated a search for new, modern and more efficient quarters. In the latter part of 1955, fortuitously, the Sheraton-Carlton Hotel decided to close its night club. This facility, consisting of a reasonably large dining room and an adjacent lounge, seemed ideal at the time. Moreover, located in mid-town in the heart of Washington's aviation activities, the Carlton had long been the unofficial headquarters of the air community.

The Carlton was happy to have a tenant and the club officials worked out an agreement with the Sheraton management. The Aviation Club would pay an annual rental fee of $10,800. The hotel would provide food and beverage service at menu prices and a percentage of the gross would be rebated to the club.

In January, 1956, the National Aviation Club abandoned the old mansion and moved into the Carlton. The attractive quarters and the convenient location of the Carlton brought an immediate and explosive increase in membership applications. Business boomed over the next two years, to the point where the club was able to repay the loans from aviation companies. With one exception: Curtiss-Wright Corporation, which had advanced $1,000, refused to accept repayment; the company's by-laws contained no provision for loans to private organizations and the Aviation Club's check would confound the bookkeeping system.

The club's quick success brought a problem. There were now several hundred members, too many for the Carlton facility which had seemed the perfect permanent headquarters only two years earlier. The dining room was overloaded at lunchtime and the member who wanted a seat in the popular lounge had to get there before noon. Barney Vierling, now president, and his colleagues decided it was time to relocate and another survey was instituted.

Sam Solomon played an indirect part in the selection of the new club quarters. His secretary at Cal-Eastern was Janice Miller, wife of Rayburn Miller, manager of the Hotel Washington. She suggested that, although the Hotel Washington had no existing facility that would serve the club's purposes, her husband might be interested in creating one. Sam relayed this possibility to Vierling and the club board and a meeting was arranged with Miller.

Miller thought that his bosses—the management of the National Hotels chain—would be willing to remodel a section of the hotel if the club would sign a long-term lease at a rate slightly higher than the Carlton rental, $12,000 a year instead of $10,800. The club's board accepted this proposal and appointed Russell B. Adams, a vice president of Pan American World Airways and also a vice president of the club, to handle the detailed negotiations with the hotel people.

After several discussions, a deal was concluded. National Hotels agreed to bear the cost of converting a portion of the Hotel Washington off the main lobby into a two-story clubhouse. The National Aviation Club signed a 10-year lease with an arrangement similar to that of the Carlton: the hotel would provide all services and rebate to the club a percentage of the sales.

The conversion took several months, during which time business continued as usual in the Carlton. Then, on July 1, 1958, the National Aviation Club moved into its beautifully-appointed new quarters in the Hotel Washington, which offered roughly double the capacity of the Carlton layout. Built at a cost of more than $350,000, the club consisted of a dining room and cocktail lounge on the first floor, and, on the second floor, a men's bar, library, board room, meeting room and game room. More than 600 people turned out for the grand opening, including the four beaming founders, who in four years had steered the NAC from its erratic infancy to status as the largest club of its type in the world.

* * * * * * * *

While Sam Solomon was devoting part of his energies to getting the Aviation Club launched, he was also busy supervising the move of the training school from Columbus Air Force Base to Moore Air Base. At Columbus, assistant director Dudley Watson, together with his principal aides, George Tennille, James McLachlen, Arthur Brown, and Chris Walk, handled the bulk of the preparatory effort. Sam continued to oversee the Columbus operation, but he focused his primary attention on making sure that the Texas base was ready at the stated time—January 3, 1955.

Sam met with the contractor in charge of rehabilitating the base and laid down the law.

"I want to make one thing absolutely clear to you," Sam said. "There will be no extras on this job, no overruns, without my express approval and my signature on the order. And I won't sign it unless it is approved in advance by Air Training Command and by the contracting officer from Air Materiel Command."

The contractor must have been impressed; there were no overruns, a real rarity on a military construction project, and the work proceeded with exceptional dispatch.

The Air Force had not allowed much time for the transfer and the necessary preliminaries, but, miraculously, Moore Air Base was ready by the end of 1954 and simultaneously Cal-Eastern's staff—part transferees from Columbus and part local people—was ready to go to work. On January 3, the target date, Cal-Eastern took over the field and a week later the first class of trainees arrived.

The training effort at Moore was the same in most respects as it had been at Columbus, but there were a couple of differences. The Beech T-34, a light indoctrination trainer for the tyro's first hours in the air, had succeeded the Cub; from there the trainee progressed to the North American T-28, a tricycle-geared, modernized and more powerful version of the T-6 used at Columbus. And the trainees were no longer cadets but student officers, coming into the Air Force already commissioned by virtue of having completed during their college years the requisite courses in the Reserve Officers Training Corps. This made no difference to Cal-Eastern's training operation but it required a substantially larger officers' club.

For a brief period in 1955, Cal-Eastern operated two Air Force schools. A decision had been made by the USAF that the final class at Columbus would complete its primary training there rather than move to Moore. That class graduated on March 12, 1955 and Cal-Eastern bade farewell to Columbus.

As he had in Columbus, Sam Solomon personally directed the community relations program at Moore except that this time it involved a triple effort; although Mission was the official home of Moore Air Base, the training field bordered on two other towns, McAllen and Edinburg. All three communities were delighted at the reactivation of the base, which brought new employment and additional sales revenue to the area, so from the beginning Sam and the Cal-Eastern team enjoyed the best of relations with the locals. With one exception; Sam himself inadvertently alienated one rancher whose property adjoined the base.

During an inspection tour of the facility, Sam had noticed that the water runoff from the sewage system was being dumped into a ditch and allowed to flow off the air base property. In an area where water was never in abundance, this seemed a great waste. He ordered that the flow be diverted back onto the base, for use in watering the new grass, shrubs and trees that had been planted. This brought a howl of outrage from the neighboring rancher, who had been using the flow to irrigate his land. He protested to Air Training Command; the complaint filtered down to Sam Solomon, who allowed it to get lost. He felt that, since the water originated on the base, it should stay there.

As the Moore Air Base operation settled into routine, Sam Solomon was active on other fronts.

Ever since Cal-Eastern had gone into the training school business, the company had been a member of the Aeronautical Training

Society, a trade association which represented all of the contract schools and other firms dealing in aviation services. In May, 1956, Solomon was elected president of the organization; he was to continue in that capacity for two years.

Since ATS was headquartered in Washington, the new post entailed no additional travel, but it did involve considerable extra work. The job was in some respects similar to the one he had held as president of the Airlines War Training Institute; the Society's principal function was serving as a liaison office between the military services and the various contractors.

For years the Society had been trying to get the Navy to contract its primary flight training, as the Air Force had so successfully done. ATS argued that the Air Force was saving millions of dollars annually by conducting its training on a contract basis, and the USAF confirmed the fact. The Navy, however, was having none of the argument; it maintained firmly that training was being handled less expensively and more efficiently by Navy instructors at Navy bases.

Under continuing pressure to effect economies wherever possible, the Navy decided to bolster its position by hiring an independent research firm to survey the situation. The seagoing service awarded the contract to Stanford Research Institute, confident that the results would justify the expenditure.

But Stanford Research rocked the boat. The reputable organization, respected for its unbiased evaluations, carefully examined the relative training approaches of the Air Force and Navy and concluded that the caliber of instruction being provided by the civilian contract schools was at least as good as the Navy's and that the contract method offered substantial savings. The report was promptly classified "top secret."

The secret was an ill-kept one, however, and the Aeronautical Training Society learned of the Stanford conclusions. The ATS board decided the time was right for another pitch to the Navy, so it directed its president to press the issue in behalf of all the contract schools. He visited offices at several levels of the Navy hierarchy, expounding on the theme of savings and efficiency through contract training. Invariably, Navy officials listened politely but made no comment.

One day, a top-echelon civilian in the Department of the Navy interrupted Solomon's presentation.

"Sam," he said, "you're wasting your time.

"Why?" Sam wanted to know.

"Because every admiral must have a station," said the Navy official, meaning that civilian takeover of the Navy's primary training would deprive the brass of a great many job "slots" that called for high rank. There were not enough top jobs as it was, and no one in the Navy was going to sponsor a program that involved elimination of more of them. Sam reluctantly accepted the fact that he could not successfully buck the system and he gave up his campaign. The Navy never did adopt the contract school approach.

Meanwhile, there had been a number of developments at California Eastern Aviation (the latter word had been substituted in the corporate title for "Airways"). Andre de Saint-Phalle had resigned as chairman of the board and he had been succeeded by Jorge Carnicero, an Argentinian who was the principal stockholder in the company's subsidiary, Air Carrier Service Corporation. Sam regretted the departure of Saint-Phalle, an able administrator and a man of vision in Sam's own mold. But he got along well with Carnicero and the change had no effect on his status in the company.

In 1956, Cal-Eastern was in good financial shape, thanks in large measure to Sam Solomon's contributions. From a minus capital position at the time he joined the company, Cal-Eastern had risen to a net worth of about $5 million and its stock had climbed from a low of three cents to about three dollars a share.

This enabled the company to embark upon a re-equipment program. In awarding contracts for domestic and international air lift, the Air Force was favoring carriers operating the newer, faster, pressurized transports that were coming off the production lines. Thus, the earning power of Cal-Eastern's old DC-4's—there were now six of them—was declining. The board voted to sell the DC-4's and to replace them with three Lockheed Super Constellations, the $6.6 million cost to be financed in part by a debenture issue. The Connies were to be delivered in mid-1957.

Coincident with the re-equipment order, Sam Solomon and Cal-Eastern's board decided to take one more crack at penetrating the Civil Aeronautics Board's resistance to certification of new scheduled carriers. There was an opportunity, Sam felt, in service between north central Texas and the West Coast, an area of mushrooming growth which was not adequately served by existing airlines. Civic leaders in the area were complaining, justifiably, that the airlines were subordinating service to their communities to primary commitments elsewhere. Too many flights touching down at their airports were already booked to capacity; travelers in the area had no alternative choices of air transportation to most points; and the airlines had not increased frequency of service in a manner corresponding to the sharply increased business and other travel needs of the area. Air coach service, in particular, was being provided on a very limited basis in the Southwest and on the West Coast.

With no scheduled service obligations elsewhere, Cal-Eastern was in a position to tailor its proposal to the requirements of the Southwest-Far West area and to offer new convenience, both in the number of flights to major cities and in service between other cities where none existed. The company filed an application with the CAB seeking authorization for a route structure that embraced the major terminals of Dallas/Fort Worth, San Diego, Los Angeles and San Francisco/Oakland, with intermediate stops at a large number of points in the southern Rocky Mountain states. The application was grouped with other requests by certificated airlines for expansion routes; the CAB designated the procedure the "Dallas to the West Case."

While the Board weighed the matter, Sam Solomon turned his attention to Cal-Eastern's most pressing problem. Land-Air, the electronics manufacturing subsidiary, had obtained a loan of several million dollars to finance its military work on aircraft and guided missiles. But the company had run into trouble and its working capital was in deficit position. The Bank of America, the lending agency, was concerned and it was about to call the loan. A credit extension was vital to Land-Air; without it the subsidiary could not continue to operate.

With Cal-Eastern controller Tom English, Sam flew to San Francisco to plead his case before top officials of the Bank of America. The Cal-Eastern duo met with Fred Ferragiero, a man Sam regarded as one of the truly outstanding people of his acquaintance. Ferragiero, executive vice president of the bank, was seconded by Neil Brogger, a vice president. The group sat down in a plush office and, with little preliminary, Ferragiero said, "Proceed, Mr. Solomon."

Sam talked steadily for half an hour, detailing the nature of Land-Air's work, its importance to the government, the prospects for future contracts and the ways by which Cal-Eastern hoped to improve the financial position of its subsidiary. Sam was not even sure that Ferragiero was listening; the executive vice president sat back in his chair, hands interlaced on his chest, staring at his fingertips. At the half-hour mark, Sam paused for comment; none was forthcoming.

Sam launched anew into his discourse, summoning every argument he could advance in favor of a credit extension. Ferragiero continued to study his fingers, his face completely devoid of expression. Finally, after more than two hours of uninterrupted speech, Sam had nothing more to add.

Sam Solomon (fourth from right, with camera) and his party, including a delegation of West German Air Force officers, inspect the flight line at Moore Air Base. Mrs. Alma Solomon is fourth from left, in dark coat. Others include Brigadier General Hannes Trautloft, head of the German delegation, third from right; J. Dudley Watson, Cal-Eastern's resident director at Moore, at Solomon's right wearing civilian clothes; and Mrs. Watson, second from right.

"That's about it," he concluded.

For a long, anxious moment, Ferragiero stared at the wall, silent. Then he turned to Neil Brogger.

"Neil, put this to the credit committee with my endorsement." That was all. Sam's eloquence had won the day and Land-Air had survived its greatest crisis.

In early 1958, Sam was at Moore Air Base, which had trained a number of German pilots, when a delegation from the German Air Force arrived for a visit. The five-man group, which was touring a number of USAF facilities, was headed by Brigadier General Hannes Trautloft, commander of the Air Training Command of the German Air Force. The delegation spent three days at the base, listening to a variety of briefings and checking out in the USAF trainers. On the last night of their stay, they expressed a desire to visit Reynosa, the Mexican town just across the border from Moore Air Base.

Sam wasn't sure about the diplomatic niceties of bringing a group of German officers into Mexico from the United States. However, he wanted to be a good host so he acceded. To be on the safe side, however, he asked that they all wear civilian clothes and that they say not a word while going through the border-crossing ceremonies. When asked if he was a citizen of the U.S., Sam responded firmly that he was, while the Germans kept silent. The immigration people were satisfied. After an exploration and shopping tour of Reynosa, the procedure was repeated and once again Sam responded for the group without challenge. Back in the U.S., Sam breathed easier. General Trautloft so much enjoyed his Moore visit, and particularly the Reynosa excursion, that he gave Sam an autographed copy of a book he had written. From that day on, Sam wondered what the book was about; it was entirely in German and the only part Sam could translate was the author's byline.

In August, 1958, Sam Solomon made a trip into yesterday, a nostalgic return to Boston where his aviation career had begun a quarter of a century earlier. The occasion was the 25th anniversary of Northeast Airlines. The company had laid on a big celebration commemorating the first passenger-carrying flights of the predecessor airline, Boston-Maine Airways, on August 11, 1933.

Northeast had grown considerably in the years since Sam had taken his leave. The airline's route structure now extended all the way to southern Florida, via Philadelphia and Washington. The personnel force had climbed from the original 10 to more than 2,400. But growth had not brought financial success; for 1958, losses would top $7 million.

The three surviving founders—Solomon, Paul Collins and Gene Vidal—joined in a cake-cutting ceremony. In the years since he had left the airline, Sam had often encountered Collins and Vidal, and their once-ruptured relations had been repaired; the three were again as friendly as they had been in the infant days of Boston-Maine Airways. Collins was now retired, Vidal a Connecticut manufacturer and a consultant to the Department of Defense; both still served on the Northeast board.

There were other old, familiar faces. Laurence Whittemore, the railroad man who had sparked the inception of the airline was on hand. Whittemore had progressed over the years to presidency of the New Haven Rail Road, a similar post with the Federal Reserve Bank of Boston, and finally to the top office of Brown Company, a leading firm in the paper industry. Milton Anderson, the first pilot, had become Northeast's chief line captain and Hazen Bean, one of the original four Boston-Maine pilots, was still flying for Northeast.

As the capper to a day of congratulations and reminiscence, the current and former Northeast officials re-flew the original route from Boston to Portland to Rockland to Bangor to Waterville and back to Boston. Milton Anderson took the controls, as he had on the first day of commercial service, but his airplane was a far throw from the old trimotor Stinson; it was a gleaming new Viscount, a four-engine British-built transport, the first of a fleet of 10 the airline had ordered. In 1933, a circuit of the route had required four and a half hours; the turboprop Viscount made it in 90 minutes.

In late 1958 and in 1959, there transpired two events which were to bring about a change of course in Sam Solomon's personal direction.

The first was the CAB's decision in the Dallas-to-the-West Case; Cal-Eastern's request for certification was once again rejected. Sam and the company's board had thought that this time they would make it, but it was not to be. It was a blow to the company, but an even greater disappointment to Sam Solomon.

Originally, Sam had joined Cal-Eastern with the hope of building another airline from scratch and of demonstrating the potential of air coach service if it were operated the way he felt it should be. The CAB action eliminated the last chance for scheduled service.

Moreover, Cal-Eastern's existing transport operations were in the decline. The Military Air Transport Service was still contracting with civilian carriers for air lift to the Far East, and also for domestic and European haulage. But MATS' appropriations for this type of service were being reduced every year. Rather than eliminate carriers which had served the military well over a long period of years, MATS was trying to spread the available contract money among a large number of operators.

Despite the introduction of the Super Constellations, Cal-Eastern was getting less and less military business and such contracts as were acquired were of a short term nature, sometimes for 90 days, sometimes only a month. The uneven utilization of the aircraft was impairing the efficiency of Cal-Eastern's Airways Division. Worse, there appeared the distinct possibility that the company might be forced out of the transport business.

The second event affected the Training Division. It was Air Force practice to contract with the civilian primary schools one year at a time on a fiscal-year basis, from July 1 to the following June 30. Ordinarily, contract renewal was simply a formality. But a development in the spring of 1959 changed the picture.

The USAF had closed one of its 11 primary training bases. The operating company, which had been in the program since its inception, was left without a school. In a conciliatory move, the USAF told the foreclosed operator that he would be given a chance to bid competitively on one of the remaining contracts. The school selected for competitive bidding was Moore Air Base, Cal-Eastern, expecting a routine renewal of its contract for the fiscal year 1960, was not prepared for the competition. It lost.

Thus, after more than eight years in the training program, during which it had graduated some 9,000 cadets and student officers at Columbus and Moore, Cal-Eastern was out in the cold. The Moore Air Base facility was turned over to the new contractor, who provided continuing employment for most of the local people. Among those who had made the transfer from Columbus, a number of the more technically qualified found positions with the Federal Aviation Administration; the others drifted off to new locales.

With the loss of the school and the threatened demise of the transport operation, Sam Solomon took stock of his own position in Cal-Eastern. The company would survive, thanks to its diversity, but Sam felt he could contribute little to the programs that now comprised the company's principal workload; maintenance and overhaul at Oakland, the widely-varied projects of the Land-Air subsidiary and the specialized, largely overseas work of Air Carrier Service Corporation. These were businesses outside the mainstream of his personal experience. It was time to bow out, Sam decided. After a full decade of service and leadership, during which he had been the principal factor in the company's rise from bankruptcy to solidity, Sam tendered his resignation.

Sam had just turned 60 but the thought of retirement never occurred to him. Retirement was for older people; Sam was a young 60. Already he was turning over in his mind an idea that had been shaping for months, a new enterprise of broad potential.

CHAPTER XIV
One More New Venture—Avemco

Sam Solomon's new venture, launched shortly after he departed Cal-Eastern, was an insurance/financing company oriented to the particular needs of the aviation community.

For some time, Sam had been interested in the possibilities of specialization and direct-sell in the insurance and financing field. Specialization, practiced by a number of existing insurance companies, made it possible to restrict clientele to the most stable elements of the community. The direct-sell technique, or bypassing the middleman, offered the added attraction of reduced cost of doing business. Together, specialization and direct-sell promised profitable operation even while providing lower rates to customers.

Why not, Sam thought, adapt this combined approach to the aviation world? The idea offered business promise and additionally it filled a need. Take, for example, the insuring and financing of general aviation aircraft, a category which embraces everything but military and commercial planes. If a general aviation flyer bought a new airplane, he usually obtained insurance and financing through the manufacturer. But the buyer of a used airplane found it difficult to get such services.

The market was much greater than anyone outside of aviation supposed. In 1959, there were more than 350,000 certificated airmen operating about 100,000 civil airplanes, the vast majority of them in the general aviation category. For personal insurance sales, there were a million employees among the principal aircraft manufacturers alone and an even larger number in the plants of the second and third tier manufacturers, suppliers of parts, equipment and services. Commercial aviation—the scheduled airlines, the supplemental carriers and certain specialized operations—added another quarter of a million.

Sam decided the promise was worth the undertaking. In November, 1959, he formed Aviation Employees Corporation, "by aviation people, for aviation people." Aviation Employees Corporation was a holding company which initially embraced two subsidiaries: Aviation Employees Insurance Company, handling aircraft insurance, and Aviation Employees Life Insurance Company. Later additions to the family included Aviation Employees Finance Company, for the financing of aircraft, and Aviation Growth

Investments, specializing in small business financing. The lengthy titles were cumbersome and they were eventually changed to "Avemco," a word-compression contributed by Alma Solomon. Avemco adopted the direct-writing principle, eliminating the in-between brokerage.

As had been the case when Sam formed Atlantic Airlines, he did not have to solicit capital. The word got around that Sam Solomon was embarking on a new venture, and a Solomon project was automatically regarded as a good investment. Initial working capital was provided by 34 investors who put up $500,000 for 250,000 shares of common stock; Sam bought in at the same price as the others, wanting no special consideration in the form of a reduced share price.

Solomon took over the Avemco presidency and a directorship and began assembling a staff. Richard E. "Dick" Fell, one of the founders of the National Aviation Club and at this time its president, became a vice president. Another vice president was Paul F. Brabazon, who had been president of Teletrip, Inc., specialists in coin-machine sales of air trip insurance. General Counsel was Joseph R. Greenwood, who had been with the Federal Power Commission and the Securities and Exchange Commission, and Emery F. Johnson, president of Air Cargo, Inc., was named treasurer.

On February 8, 1960, Avemco filed a registration statement with the Securities and Exchange Commission for proposed $5 million financing. The money was to be raised by sale of 2-1/2 million shares of common stock, the issue to be handled by two underwriters, one in Washington and one in New York, both specialists in insurance stock.

For re-insurance, Sam went to England and presented his case to Lloyd's of London. Avemco, like any small insurance company, could only carry a certain amount of insurance and policies written beyond that amount had to be backed by a major company such as Lloyd's. At first, Lloyd's was reluctant to accept Sam's proposal; the firm's officials didn't like what they considered a high accident rate in general aviation flying in the United States. In the end, Sam's personal reputation and his record of accomplishment won out, as it had on several occasions in his past.

Avemco started operations in a downtown Washington office but moved within a few months to Silver Spring, Maryland, not far from Sam Solomon's home. The building had been vacated by a Sam Snead indoor golf school and the school had left behind its putting practice green. In remodeling the building for office use, Sam directed that the green be kept intact as part of the reception area,

A big step in the life of Avemco, the aviation insurance firm founded by Sam Solomon, was conclusion of an agreement whereby the company became official insurer for the 180,000-member Aircraft Owners and Pilots Association. Here Solomon (right) and AOPA president J. B. Hartranft, Jr. put their signatures to the agreement.

for the amusement of visiting businessmen and clients. Avemco's expense record contained a notation for "Putters and golf balls," and the company thereby scored what was undoubtedly a "first" in the insurance industry.

In the beginning, the business failed by a large margin to meet Sam's expectations. The life insurance program was something of a disaster. Aircraft insurance fared little better initially, but Avemco's future brightened considerably when Sam negotiated a deal whereby the company became the official insurer for the Aircraft Owners and Pilots Association, a nationwide organization boasting a roster of some 180,000 members. That set Avemco on the road to solidity.

Meanwhile, Sam had continued active in the affairs of the National Aviation Club. In October, 1960, he was elected president, thus becoming the last of the founding foursome to assume the top office.

Later that year, just after Christmas, Sam suffered a serious heart attack, apparently induced by the heavy workload connected with the founding and early operation of Avemco. He spent two weeks in the hospital and several more weeks recuperating at home. His enforced idleness caused him to miss President John F. Kennedy's inaugural parade and brought to an end an extraordinary record. Until that time, Sam had attended every inaugural parade in the 20th century, starting with that of William McKinley in 1901, when Sam was taking his first steps, and continuing through the second inauguration of Dwight D. Eisenhower.

In October, 1961, Sam was re-elected president of the National Aviation Club, which had been booming ever since its move to the Hotel Washington. Membership had topped the 2,100 mark, a near-saturation point, and rebates from the hotel had swelled the club's coffers. The NAC was thus in a position to provide funding for a number of worthwhile aviation projects. In one such instance, the club donated $20,000 to buy, for the Smithsonian Institution's National Air Museum, one of the world's most comprehensive collections of aviation books, 1,400 volumes dating back to 1784. In another, the NAC financed the travels of an aviation sport group.

The latter incident occurred in the summer of 1962, when Sam Solomon's second tour as president was drawing to a close. There was to be an international aerobatic competition in Budapest, Hungary, and a team composed of the best of the United States' acrobatic flyers had been formed to carry the American flag in the air Olympics. The team had sought government help to defray the costs of the trip, but none had been forthcoming. The National Aviation Club came to the rescue; its board of governors voted to put up the money for the team's expenses and additionally directed that the club president accompany the group to spread the NAC's prestige abroad.

It was Sam's first trip to Budapest and he thoroughly enjoyed the Hungarian capital with its old world charm and its many beautiful parks fringing the fabled Danube, which flows a curving course through the center of the city. Hungary, of course, was Iron Curtain territory and in 1962 the cold war had not yet thawed. But Sam found none of the hostility and suspicion an American behind the curtain might expect to encounter. To the contrary, he was treated royally. He had even been provided his own retainer, a little man who guided Sam wherever he went, served as interpreter, arranged for cars when they were needed and who, even when Sam was in his hotel, always hovered in the background ready to do Sam's bidding.

Sam commented on Hungarian hospitality to Jacques Allez, president of the Federation Aeronautique Internationale, the organization which sanctioned and refereed world-wide aviation records and contests.

"They've even given me a personal aide," Sam related to Allez, describing the services of his little man.

Allez roared.

"Sam, my infant," he said, "they are simply keeping watch on you."

Sam's long interest in helicopters, which had been born almost as early as the helicopter itself, prompted his investment, in 1963, in a new company which proposed to operate helicopters in the Washington-Baltimore area. Sam bought stock with his own money and in addition sponsored an Avemco small business loan to Washington-Baltimore Helicopter Company. The company had secured a contract to operate the helicopter traffic observation service in Washington and it had filed an application with the Civil Aeronautics Board for a scheduled service between downtown areas of both cities and their three airports. The application, unfortunately, was never approved; the CAB took a dim view of regular helicopter service, in light of the experiences of operators who had tried it, and the noise considerations of town-center operation were another minus. Sam was elected to the board of directors of Washington-Baltimore Helicopter, but he did not take an active part in the company's management.

Meanwhile, Avemco was weathering a succession of storms, never in dire straits but neither enjoying business prosperity. The planned $5 million financing had never materialized; the stock issue had netted only slightly more than $2 million. This deprived the company of the large reserves needed for insurance programs. Life insurance sales remained low, but even if life business had boomed Avemco would not have been able to handle it; the life insurance company was sold. By 1965, things settled to the point where Avemco could be termed a success; the company was breaking no industry records but it had achieved a solid foundation for future growth.

On July 1, 1965, Sam Solomon stepped down from the presidency. There was a proposal by some board members to oppose his re-election; Alexander G. Hardy, a former vice president of National Airlines, a member of the Avemco board since the company's founding and a competent executive, was available for the job and he had backing.

Sam was not of a mind to contest the proposal. He had reached what others considered the normal retirement age of 65 and he felt he had run his course with Avemco. Sam had provided the spark of life for the company; he had done a good job of organizing it, putting the right people in the right jobs; he had personally concluded the most important deal of the company's early years, the arrangement with the Aircraft Owners and Pilots Association that was to be the cornerstone of the company's business.

But he admitted to some mistakes and some omissions; there had never been enough money to do the things he wanted to do. He felt that his record of administration with regard to the life insurance and health-accident insurance programs had left something to be desired. In short, Sam's forte was vision and planning, but what the company needed most at this time was a hard-nosed, pragmatic, day-to-day administrator of top caliber. Thus, in the interests of company harmony, Sam informed the board that he would not be a candidate for re-election. Alexander Hardy was elected president and Sam remained with Avemco as a member of the board.

Retirement age or no, Sam Solomon had no intention of taking to the rocking chair. His lack of a regular business occupation gave him time to devote to a project which had been on his mind for some time: a concept for a solution to aviation's big and growing problem of time-consuming travel to and from airports.

Sam's concern with this problem had originated as far back as his period as manager of Washington-Hoover Airport. Washington-Hoover, only a little more than two miles from downtown Washington, had been a gem as far as traveler convenience was concerned; with one possible exception, it had been closer to the center of action than any other major city airport in the United States. But it was about that time that a trend started: airports began moving farther and farther from the cities they served.

By 1965, when Sam Solomon refocused his attention on the problem, the situation was reaching ridiculous proportions. Overall time from departure point to destination, much of it spent in ground travel, was eroding the major advantage of air transportation—rapidity of movement. A Boston official, commenting on a plan to build a new airport to serve the city, dryly stated that the "nearest site appears to be in Wyoming."

The reason airports were moving farther away, of course, was the fact that airplanes were continually getting bigger and faster and noisier; they needed more runway room for landings and take-offs, more unobstructed area around the airport for departures and approaches. The only way to get the requisite clear space was to move out into the country, hence the problem.

The solution, as Sam saw it, was to separate short-haul air transportation from medium/long-haul flight. Long distance planes would continue to use the way-out airports but short-haul craft, operating within a radius of 250 miles or so, would fly directly to and from mid-town airports. The inner city airfield would be connected to the long-haul airports either by a rapid transit system or by short-haul aircraft.

The prime needs for such a concept were a specially designed downtown terminal and a short-haul airplane capable of carrying a moderately large passenger payload—40 to 50 people—yet still able to land and take off from a runway no longer than 1,000 feet.

Other than to cite general requirements, Sam did not intend to offer specifications for the design of the airplanes; that was for others more competent in the field, and in 1966 there was already under way a considerable research and development effort on planes capable of very-short-field operation. It included large passenger helicopters and compound helicopters (those with wings and a separate propulsion system for faster forward speed); short take-off and landing aircraft, or STOL's in industry parlance, planes with specially designed wings and other lifting devices which dramatically shortened runway roll; and vertical take-off and landing aircraft, or VTOL's, craft equipped with lift-jets for taking off straight up and with jet cruise engines for normal flight. All of these types could operate within a thousand feet of runway with a generous safety margin left over.

These planes, Sam fully realized, would not be available for regular service in the immediate or even in the near-future. But one did not wait until the airplane is ready, then start work on the other element of the system. A lot of study and thought had to go into the downtown terminal, which in itself would take a minimum of five

Artist's conception of the "Airport in the Sky," a downtown V/STOLport proposed by Sam Solomon in February, 1967.

years to complete even after an efficient design had been established.

It was on this area that Sam focused his attention, but not with the idea of turning it into monetary gain for himself. He planned to make his work available to the government and the air world; it would, he thought, perhaps be his last contribution to the aviation industry in which he had worked for more than three decades.

Sam embarked first on a careful study of all the factors involved in operating a midtown airport—and there were many. In the course of his work, he advised Federal Aviation Administration officials what he had in mind and they invited him to witness a practical demonstration of short-field performance. At a special air show in New York, called Metro '66, the FAA put several of the newly-developed STOL aircraft through their paces; operating at relatively low noise levels, they took off and landed on a street, a pier and a small park in lower Manhattan. It was a very impressive demonstration, a preview of things to come. It didn't seem to impress the blase New Yorkers very much, Sam noted; at the park, those who bothered to watch did so with no visible trace of excitement and a group of youngsters playing nearby didn't even bother to look when a STOL plane got off the ground in less than the length of a football field.

Sam got some first-hand knowledge of STOL capabilities when he flew from the pier as a passenger in a Fairchild Turbo-Porter, an eight-place light turboprop. After a brief flight, the pilot started to descend to a landing on the pier. Sam looked out the window and studied the pier; from his altitude it looked like a postage stamp, although it was about a thousand feet long. Sam was convinced that it was impossible to set an airplane down on that short strip, but the Porter touched down gently and came to a halt in a surprisingly short time. The landing roll had taken, Sam estimated, no more than 200 feet, only a fifth of the distance that was considered reasonable for a safe STOL runway.

After completing the study phase in 1966, Sam hired an architect, John Samperton, who had worked for Solomon once before in the distant past. Sam, when he was manager of Washington-Hoover Airport, had hired young Samperton as a locker-room attendant at the airport swimming pool. Together they drew up detailed plans for a number of terminal structures and obtained patents on them.

In February, 1967, Sam made the terminal plan public. "Airport in the Sky," he called it, for the key to the design was a landing platform far above street level, built atop a hotel or office complex.

There were good reasons for elevating the runway. First, the airport had to be self-supporting. A surface level downtown airport existing solely on landing fees could never in a hundred years pay back the cost of razing extremely valuable business property. By elevating the landing field, the space beneath could be utilized for a variety of purposes: bus terminal, hotel, offices, shops, all of them producing revenue for the airport operator, be it commercial firm or the municipality. This would also produce tax revenue for the city.

The other reason was the technical consideration: if the landing field were at surface level the surrounding buildings would obstruct the flight path of landing STOLs and cause too steep an angle of descent for safe operation; thus the runway had to be at a height commensurate with the adjacent structures. This would not be practicable in skyscraper areas, of course, but even in "stone canyon" cities like New York and Chicago there were close-in places where the Airport in the Sky could be constructed. Sam cited examples: over the piers in New York, over the railroad tracks in Chicago.

"Ultimately air service must be provided from where you want to leave to where you want to go," read Solomon's presentation, "which basically is from inner city to inner city.

"Airport in the Sky is an imaginative approach to the airport problem, no longer limited to expanding the size of airports, length of runways, and renovating terminal buildings at tremendous expense. It is an airport designed for the convenience of the passenger and not designed principally for the airplane operating over longer and longer ranges and non-stop distances."

As an illustration, Sam provided details of a skyport structure designed for use in Washington, D.C. It would cover roughly six city blocks in the midtown area. The topmost level of the structure would be the landing field, containing only a control tower and a 1,000-foot runway; runway elevation would be approximately the 10-story level, as high or higher than the surrounding rooftops.

After landing, the helicopter, STOL or VTOL would taxi to an elevator similar to those used on aircraft carriers and descend one level to discharge its passengers. This level, protected from the elements by the landing platform above, would be the terminal proper. It would contain parking spaces for the aircraft at loading gates, along with aircraft servicing facilities and all the apparatus of an airport—ticket counters, insurance counters, car rental counters, food and cocktail service, employee cafeteria, newsstands, barber shops, telephones, baggage rooms and conveyor belts for baggage, toilets, and so forth.

On the several floors below the terminal level, there would be offices or hotel rooms or a combination of both—hundreds of them because the runway length requirement necessarily made the structure rather large. At ground level, there would be a bus terminal, ringed by shops. Below ground, there would be several levels of parking space.

The public announcement of the concept received wide publicity, abroad as well as in the United States. Sam subsequently obtained three patents on the airport design and announced that they were available free of charge to anyone who might want to pursue the idea. He talked with a number of government officials, who displayed mild interest, but most felt that the idea was ahead of its time; in Washington, almost every idea is ahead of its time and that is particularly true in aviation, where the government's area of responsibility for flight has often failed to keep pace with technological advance.

The Airport in the Sky languished until February, 1972, when Sam brought it up again in conversation with Charles Carey, a deputy FAA administrator. Carey thought that his boss, FAA Administrator John Shaffer, should hear of the plan; he arranged a meeting. To Shaffer, Sam outlined the essentials of his concept; the Administrator asked that Sam leave with him a drawing of the design, but otherwise he was noncommittal. Sam heard no more, from Shaffer or his aides.

Five months later, in July, 1972, the Federal Aviation Administration issued a press release to the effect that it was going to study the "elevated STOLport" to be "located on top of a multi-level structure." It was awarding a $199,249 contract to Parsons, Brinckeroff, Quade and Douglas, Inc., a New York architectural and engineering firm, for design and cost estimates.

There was no mention of Sam Solomon's prior work. In fact, the FAA didn't even send him a copy of the press release. He got one through the mail from Albert "Abbie" Wolf, a retired general who was attorney for the Aircraft Owners and Pilots Association.

"This sounds somewhat familiar to me," Wolf scrawled on an accompanying note.

Sam accepted the FAA's slight philosophically. He had, after all, offered the Airport in the Sky design to anyone interested. The important thing was the fact that the FAA now thought enough of the idea to spend a substantial amount of money for a new survey of the possibilities. Sam was confident that, although the originator's identity might get lost in the shuffle, the Airport in the Sky would become an important adjunct of tomorrow's aviation.

CHAPTER XV
Some Views of a Pioneer

Just after Christmas, 1973, Sam and Alma Solomon celebrated their golden wedding anniversary. Some 300 friends and relatives joined in the celebration and among the gathering there were many who had worked with, for or against Sam Solomon during various phases of his multi-faceted career. The occasion prompted a flood of reminiscences about the airline, Sam's hectic days at Washington-Hoover Airport and all the other ventures in which he had engaged over the years.

Washington-Hoover Airport, of course, had long since vanished. The land it had once occupied was now partly Potomac parkland, partly the approaches and parking lots of the massive Pentagon.

Northeast Airlines no longer existed as an entity, but its spirit was still flying the airways. In 1972, Northeast had been merged into one of the world's largest carriers, Delta Air Lines.

Atlantic Airlines was gone, too, but it had left a valuable legacy to commercial air transportation. Sam Solomon's first application for air coach service had pointed the way for a gradually accelerating transition toward reduced fare levels. In 1973, economy and special-inducement fares accounted for more than 80 percent of the revenues of the U.S. scheduled airlines.

In his original operational plan for Atlantic Airlines, Solomon had proposed to provide "all the way" service to and from hundreds of communities which had no kind of air service whatever. His total trip concept had included provision of bus transportation, connecting these communities with airports on Atlantic Airlines' routes. That was the first time anyone had ever considered the transport needs of small towns; until then, the attitude of the carriers had generally been "Get to the air route stop any way you can." Sam's idea served as a pathfinder for a later adaptation of the total trip concept made possible by advancing technology. Outlying communities are now served by "third-level" or "commuter" airlines, flying light transports to and from the terminals on the regular routes of the major carriers.

The training and transport programs of Cal-Eastern to which Sam had devoted 10 years of effort were no longer extant, but the company was very much alive and well. Now called Dynalectron Corporation, it was a large complex of enterprises, engaged in such varied pursuits as aircraft and missile maintenance, missile range operations, international marketing of aviation equipment and manufacture of electronics and electro-mechanical equipment.

The National Aviation Club, which Sam had helped create, was approaching its 20th year, no longer as prosperous as it had been in the boom years of the latter '50s and the early '60s but nonetheless operationally solid. The club had moved from the Hotel Washington to a midtown location in 1968, had survived a membership exodus in the aviation recession of 1970, and was beginning to build anew.

Avemco, now located in Bethesda, Maryland, was very much a going concern, the largest insurer of general aviation aircraft in the world, also a high-volume financier of non-airline planes.

Sam and Alma Solomon were still living in the Silver Spring home they had first occupied 45 years earlier. They were alone in the big house now; their three sons had married and moved away, although all were living in the Silver Spring area, which made it convenient for the elder Solomons to visit their eight grandchildren.

Sam no longer had a regular aviation occupation, but he maintained a degree of aviation activity through his memberships on various boards: Avemco; the former Washington-Baltimore Helicopter Company, which had become Pioneer Industries; and the National Aviation Club, which had given him lifetime board status as a Governor Emeritus. Through extensive reading and almost daily visits to the club, an unofficial center of information about the latest doings of the aviation fraternity, Sam managed to stay abreast of developments.

Speaking from the vantage point of four decades' experience, Sam had some anniversary comments on the state of aviation.

"I don't think the scheduled airline industry is doing enough to induce people to travel," he said. "With modern airplane development, it is possible to build transports of greater and greater seat capacity. The airlines should be taking advantage of this potential, trying to fill those seats. There are still millions of people who have never flown and they should be the principal targets of airline advertising and promotion. Instead, the scheduled carriers are content to let the supplementals develop the first-timer market while they—the certificated carriers—waste their promotional energies trying to take passengers away from each other. They focus on those who are already flying, rather than those who never have and that retards real growth."

Also, Sam said, he still feels the airlines could go further toward the elimination of frills, particularly meal service, as he first proposed to do in 1945.

"I saw an ad recently which boasted a choice of three main courses in coach and five in first class. That points up the extremes airlines go to in order to lure passengers away from each other. Perhaps, on a long overwater flight, the passengers really need meal service, but they don't need it—and I'm sure most don't care about it—on a one-hour domestic flight. The airlines are spending millions of dollars on meal service—for the meals themselves, people to prepare them, people to deliver them to the airplane and people to serve them. They would do better to eliminate meals on domestic flights and pass the saving on to the passenger in the form of a reduced fare."

Solomon on the controversial American supersonic transport:

"I am confident that there will someday be an American SST in the air. The original version was killed in a wave of hysteria, by people who didn't have the facts right but managed to convince others that they did. We should remember that we, as Americans, do not have the power of life or death over aviation progress. If we abdicate—as we did temporarily in the initial SST cancellation—other nations will be glad of the opportunity to benefit.

"The British, French and Russians are flying their SSTs, and despite a rash of sales problems with the Concords, these planes will be flying passengers—and flying them to the United States, as well. They are not the last word in supersonic flight; but they will most likely whet the passenger's appetite for greater speed and convenience, as has every generation of airlines.

"There is also the economic reason. An American SST represents potential billions in sales and of special importance is sales to foreign carriers. I think most of the objections to the SST will be overcome by continuing research and by enlightenment—people will come to realize that a supersonic airplane is not the monstrous thing its detractors would have us believe. The combination of passenger demand and economic potential will revive the American SST."

About aircraft noise:

"I think the aviation industry has done a terrible public relations job on the noise matter. Actually, the trend of the early '60s toward louder airplanes has been reversed; even though their engines are much more powerful, the newer airplanes coming off the production lines, like the DC-10 or L-1011, are a great deal quieter than the first generation of jetliners. There's a lot of research going on in this area, and I'm sure airplanes will become a lot less noisy than they are today.

"But, let's face it, you don't get a half million pounds of airplane off the ground without making some noise. We've never eliminated truck or train noise, and we are not going to eliminate airplane noise. The airplane is not going to be eliminated, either, no matter how loudly the environmentalists scream; it is an integral part of our commerce and our economy.

"People must acknowledge that and accept the fact that noise is a way of life. Sometimes the birds wake me up in the morning, but I don't consider that a reason for eliminating birds."

Solomon's views in an area in which he has special expertise, short-haul air transportation:

"High-capacity STOL and VTOL airlines—I'm speaking of 40 to 50, possibly up to 100, seats—have not come into being as rapidly as they might have. One of the reasons is that there has been no willingness to plunge in and actually start development, although everyone seems to agree that there is a need for this type of airplane. The costs of developing new aircraft have risen out of sight and a single manufacturer can no longer afford a project like this, nor can he obtain outside financing because of the risk.

"There is under way a lot of research and development effort, here and abroad, on airframes and engines and even complete STOL/VTOL aircraft. These planes have been on the horizon a long time, but it seems the horizon is getting closer. In the United States, however, these projects are military oriented and although we are being told that they are being developed with an eye to civilian-use adaptability, I wonder about that.

"Take, for example, the Air Force project called AMST (for Advanced Medium STOL). This is an airplane designed to operate in forward combat areas where there are no prepared strips, but the Air Force feels you can always find as much as 2,000 feet of landing space available. The airplane is being designed with that as a target.

"But where can you find that much space in a city? Even using the elevated structure approach, building atop other facilities, 2,000 feet is hard to come by. I still feel that 1,000 feet is the maximum practicable if one contemplates locating the airport within the city.

"I feel that the government should take over the matter of developing both the STOL/VTOL airplane and the midtown airport into which it can operate. Call it an 'aviation Amtrak.' In Amtrak, the government is subsidizing railroad passenger service which the railroads would otherwise abandon. It is an investment in efficient transportation for the taxpayer. Why not make it really efficient and provide *air* transportation from city center to city center? The Federal Aviation Administration finally appears to be taking the midtown airport seriously; hopefully the government will realize that it is time to think of the airplane to go with it, a STOL/VTOL designed expressly for civil use and not a military castoff.

"If the government does take some action in this area, I am confident that the evolving airport will be an elevated, multi-level, self-supporting structure such as I visualized in 1967. I feel now, as I did then, that the Airport in the Sky, serviced by short-haul transports that can operate within an extremely short runway length, is the soundest approach to a really efficient air transportation system."

One of aviation's greatest needs is men of vision, according to Solomon.

"I frequently read of the great vision on the part of aviation men in the past. There was some, of course, but in 40 years of personal experience I encountered remarkably few men of vision. I think there are fewer today.

"I find an example in current agreements among the airlines and the Civil Aeronautics Board involving limitations of service. Faced with overcapacity on certain routes, more seats available than can be filled, the airlines have come up with what they consider a solution: reducing the number of flight schedules as an economy measure. This gives them a higher load factor, a greater percentage of available seats filled, on the remaining flights.

"But what they are doing is depriving the flying public of choice. By limiting flight frequencies, they are taking away some of the convenience of air travel. This is not an answer to their economic problems. It is a shortsighted measure which seeks to cure the symptoms rather than the cause of the economic illness.

"The answer is to develop new traffic, to reach and sell the vast market of people who have never flown at all. That's how you build a really effective air transportation system, not by patching current problems at the expense of public service."

Finally, Solomon on Solomon:

"I have had a wonderful, very diversified career, full of interest. There have been failures, but I think they were outweighed by the successes.

"I managed to become involved in so many things I knew nothing about. But I had one thing going for me: I always knew before anyone else how much I didn't know."